Jesus the Everlasting
Hope of Humankind

Jesus the Everlasting Hope of Humankind

*Biblical Theology Prompted by Visions
and Dreams from the Holy Spirit*

Don Elijah Eckhart

RESOURCE *Publications* · Eugene, Oregon

Resource Publications
An Imprint of Wipf and Stock Publishers
199 W. 8th Ave., Suite 3
Eugene, OR 97401

www.wipfandstock.com

PAPERBACK ISBN: 978-1-5326-4802-1
HARDCOVER ISBN: 978-1-5326-4803-8
EBOOK ISBN: 978-1-5326-4804-5

Manufactured in the U.S.A.   AUGUST 24, 2018

To those Christians
who have been called
to "not quench the Spirit"
while questioning traditions.

Contents

Acknowledgements

WHILE MANY PEOPLE HAVE given constructive comments about this undertaking, I am especially grateful to two individuals for their help in the completion of this book. I appreciate the valuable input given to me by both James Goetz and Dr. Brenda Colijn. Their encouragement has also meant much to me along the way.

James Goetz, who is an independent scholar and author of *Conditional Futurism: New Perspectives of End-Time Prophecy*, has worked with me as a developmental editor for the last four years to turn this work into a publishable book. We shared ideas and *discussed* them *long distance* using email between my home in Columbus, Ohio, and his in Liverpool, New York. My wife Sue Ellen and I were blessed to meet James and his wife Laurie before working in earnest to transform this project into a book. James also did the copyediting and was instrumental in the final phases that led to the book actually being published.

Brenda B. Colijn, Ph.D., who is Professor of Biblical Interpretation and Theology at Ashland Theological Seminary and author of *Images of Salvation in the New Testament*, was my advisor for my first version of this work, which was completed in 2013 as my master's thesis. Not only is Dr. Colijn adept at theological concepts, she is skilled at grammar. Both skills were very helpful as I worked toward completing my thesis. Dr. Colijn also taught theology courses which were of great help for me to understand the bigger picture of theological concepts emanating from biblical interpretation.

My gratitude extends to the many faculty members of Ashland Theological Seminary who reviewed my research papers and offered helpful comments as I was seeking truth from the Bible and from Christians who have gone before. The list of faculty who were especially helpful in my search for answers include Rev. Thomas A. Snyder, Dr. Onalee J. Pierce, Dr. JoAnn Ford Watson, Dr. Wyndy Corbin Reusching, and Dr. Paul W. Chilcote.

1

Revelation of Purification
in Life and Afterlife

I WAS NOT DISOBEDIENT TO THE HEAVENLY VISION. . . .
(ACTS 26:19 NEW REVISED STANDARD VERSION)

Introduction

I ENROLLED IN SEMINARY because of a song—but not just any song. With
the tune of the old hymn "Beneath the Cross of Jesus" playing in my head,[1]
new words came to my mind in the early morning of Holy Saturday, April
3, 1999. I arose from my bed and wrote down those words. That morning,
I heard them for the first time, and I knew they came from God, not me.
The Lord called me and led me to examine the biblical basis for the ideas
in this revelation:

> Beyond the cross of Jesus, I cannot bear to see,
> The sight of that dear dying man Who gave His life for me;
> And when the picture quickly fades, I see the risen Christ,
> The One for Whom I'll die myself, greets me saying "Arise!"
> (Verse 1)

1. Words by Elizabeth C. Clephane in 1868 and music by Frederick C. Maker in 1881.

1

Upon the cross of Jesus, for sin His blood was poured;
His love a sacrifice for all, Christ is my Living Lord;
So as my life has grown with Him, the story to be told;
The One for Whom I've died myself, the first for me to hold.
(Verse 2)

What if I'd never known Him, what would "eternal" be?
Would I be drowning deep inside, within a fiery sea?
If I could gasp for one last breath, to utter one last word,
From deep within my soul I'd cry to God just for "mercy."
(Verse 3)

If God could hear me calling, I know He'd grant my plea;
But how much longer would it be until He rescues me?
And then a figure comes in view—who could this savior be?
He's Jesus Christ, my Servant King—the God I long to see!!!
(Verse 4)

I gave a title to the new revelatory song: "Beyond the Cross of Jesus—Christ Greets Me." The song divides into two parts. Verses 1 and 2 reflect a life devoted to Jesus Christ and eternal life which flows naturally from earthly life—unbroken by death. I will call this person *Adjoined*. The name reflects an individual who is aligned with Jesus; that is, the person believes and obeys Christ. Verses 3 and 4 represent a person who is lost and experiencing eternal punishment. I will call this individual *Alone* because of the solitary state in which the person exists. Totally helpless, this person is in despair until calling to God for "mercy." Then, Jesus saves the wretched soul from the fiery sea.

The title "Beyond the Cross of Jesus—Christ Greets Me" applies to both the first two verses (salvation during this lifetime) and the last two verses (showing how salvation could be possible through Christ after this life). In verses 1 and 2, followers of Christ are *beyond* the cross historically yet walk with Jesus and are guided by the Holy Spirit every day. In verses 3 and 4, lost persons are oftentimes thought to be *beyond* the redemption of Jesus' sacrifice. A weighty question is asked: "What if I'd never known Him, what would 'eternal' be?" It essentially asks: If I had never come to faith in Jesus Christ, what would be my eternal fate? It also asks about the eternal destiny of all people of all times and all places. *Eternal* is a key word; I did not know its full significance at the time I wrote down these verses.

However, as I have found in my studies, its meaning helps to demonstrate that no one is *beyond* the salvation made possible by Jesus Christ.

Have misgivings? I did. That is not how the Bible is generally read—that is, according to how *most* Christians understand it or have been told what the Bible means. "Once someone dies, that's the end—heaven or hell," most preachers say. "No one gets a 'second chance,'" they say to emphasize the point. "Hell is everlasting conscious torment," asserts the evangelist; "say a prayer while you can still be saved." I relate to these concerns. Before Holy Saturday 1999, I would never have considered the possibility that Jesus saves in *eternity* and that God wants to save everyone. Even after the revelation of the song, I did not know what to do with it.

At that point, I was a lifelong Christian who experienced a personal spiritual awakening in the spring 1972 during my senior year of college. Sue Ellen and I married on August 19, 1972. Then, I completed a Master of Public Administration at the University of Pennsylvania; began a career in budgeting and policy analysis for local governments and later a state government; became a father of two sons; and volunteered with local church ministries before God gave me a revelation in 1985. Then, I received more revelations starting in 1996 and the revelation on Holy Saturday 1999.

I contemplated the revelatory song for several years. After I retired from my thirty-year career in government budgeting, I enrolled in seminary and completed a master's degree in Christian theology. The classes and thesis focused on biblical studies, theology, and church history. Since there was no specific curriculum on the possibility of salvation after death, I did research papers and special projects on particular aspects of this scarcely studied subject. I diligently prayed and studied whether my revelation is biblical and true. Let us return to the song in order to understand it more fully before proceeding.

Faith Demonstrated in the Revelation

The first two verses of the song depict a person who has devoted their life to the Lord Jesus Christ, but not all at once. The person envisions Jesus dying on the cross, and the person believes that Jesus "gave His life for me." Then, the person envisions the risen Christ and believes that Jesus is the *way* to eternal life. At the end of verse 1, the person makes a commitment to Christ, "The One for Whom I'll die myself." The now devout follower of Christ figuratively dies by giving up their self-centered life and living in obedience to Jesus. For example, Jesus said, "Those who want to save their life will lose it, and *those who lose their life for my sake, and for the sake of the gospel, will save it*" (Mark 8:34–35 NRSV, *emphasis added*). By giving up our self-centered life, we find true life in Christ.

Similarly, Jesus said, "If any want to become my followers, let them deny themselves and take up their cross daily and follow me" (Luke 9:23 NRSV). The concept of *taking up one's cross* is also figurative for dying to a self-centered life. Jesus in this verse emphasized that death-to-self is ongoing, and so is life in Christ. A sacrificial life serves a purpose beyond oneself. For example, Paul wrote: "For while we live, we are always being given up to death for Jesus' sake, so that the life of Jesus may be made visible in our mortal flesh. So death is at work in us, but life in you" (2 Cor 4:11–12 NRSV).

In verse 2, the person gains a better understanding of Jesus' sacrifice of himself on the cross—"His love a sacrifice for all." Such great, selfless love brings a response, "Christ is my Living Lord." To be Lord means to be Master—a relationship that is often lost in contemporary Christianity which thrives on grace. For Jesus to be Lord means that the person will obey Jesus' commands. Indeed, we see that in the song: "So as my life has grown with Him, the story to be told." Now we can see why this person is called *Adjoined*. He or she has joined Christ in the abundant life (John 10:10), fulfilling God-given purposes and serving others for Christ, "The One for Whom I've died myself." The story points to the gracious work of Jesus Christ.

On the other side is *Alone*, described in verses 3 and 4 of the song. This person either did not believe in Jesus or did not even know who Jesus is. To a certain branch of traditional theology called *restrictivism* and the traditional Western Christian doctrine of hell, it makes no difference if Alone rejected belief in Christ or never heard of Christ because all people in either situation are damned forever. That is not at all the position of this revelatory song and book. In verse 3, it is apparent that Alone is struggling within himself or herself—the struggle may be with sins against God and against people—sins now seen for the harm caused. A battle between self-will (perhaps self-righteousness) and a new attitude is now waging within Alone. It feels like the old self is drowning out any possibility of a fresh start. Yet the fire in that sea is purifying Alone. No excuses, no blaming others will do. The sins are to be borne alone—at least that is what Alone now feels. However, the burden becomes too much! Alone cries out to God for "mercy." Suddenly, Alone receives assurance.

Alone now believes that if God could hear him or her calling, God would "grant my plea." At this point, we may note that faith has been sparked or rekindled in Alone. However, he or she will remain alone for an unknown duration. Salvation comes by the only way to the Father, that is, by Jesus Christ, who is both "Servant" and "King." No longer alone, the one who *once was lost but now is found* is welcomed into the presence of God.

Both Adjoined and Alone are saved by grace through faith. The devotion that characterizes Adjoined is nurtured by the Holy Spirit throughout Adjoined's life as a believer. However, it is for Adjoined to demonstrate faith during his or her life. On the other hand, Alone demonstrated faith only in the most dire of circumstances, after suffering the torment of seeing the negative, even devastating, effects of sins and lack of forgiveness toward others. Obviously, Adjoined enjoys an incomparably better life after death than does Alone. The same was true of Adjoined during this earthly life.

Jesus' death on the cross compensated for the sins of everyone in the world. Nonetheless, each person must acknowledge that he or she is a sinner and turn away from sin. When someone believes in Jesus, the Holy Spirit works in the person, and as in the case of Adjoined, the person is purified during this lifetime. No longer does sin hold any attraction. If Adjoined does sin, he or she confesses it to God and makes it right to any offended person. Adjoined is prepared to enter heaven with Jesus there to greet his faithful one.

On the other hand, after an exhausting experience in the lake of fire which seemed to have no end, Alone believes in Jesus and has been purified as much as people who believe in Jesus during their earthly life. No longer alone, this restored person joins the ranks of the redeemed in relationship with God and in fellowship with other people. Both Adjoined and Alone have come to faith in Jesus by their human free will. Granted, it took a hellish situation for Alone to come to that realization. Nevertheless, by this song of revelation, we can see how God's desire that everyone be saved can actually happen.

Can the Good News Be Even Better than We Thought?

The effects of this revelation are wide-reaching yet not complicated. Two parallel themes flow through Scripture: one, personal faith in the Lord Jesus Christ is essential for salvation; and the other, God wants all to be saved. A dilemma exists: with justification by faith necessary for salvation, can everyone be saved? Church doctrines typically state or imply that both themes cannot be entirely true, predominately concluding that not all will be saved. The research in this book shows how both themes can actually occur—true to God's word.

The traditional Western Christian doctrine of salvation says that the opportunity to believe in Jesus Christ ceases upon a person's death. In this revelation, each person faces judgment; however, eternal punishment is not endless as tradition has contended. The traditional view has led churches and Christian groups to unduly focus on conversion and to neglect teaching the full meaning of discipleship. Proclaiming the gospel is unquestionably vital to the mission of the church. However, focusing exclusively on conversion, especially with repeated appeals to convert, can lead to a fear of damnation. Fear does not result in disciples who are fully devoted to the Lord Jesus Christ. Rather, such devotion comes from voluntary submission to Jesus, as guided by the work of the Holy Spirit.

The significance of this subject is witnessed in countries where Christianity is growing dramatically, for example, in Africa, Asia, and Latin America. First-generation Christians wonder about the eternal destiny of their parents, grandparents and other ancestors who did not know of Christ or did not believe in him as Savior and Lord. Alternatively, parents and grandparents in countries where Christianity is declining, such as in Europe and to a lesser extent in America, may be concerned about the eternal destiny of their children and grandchildren. Furthermore, this revelation may resonate with the views of Native Americans, former Muslims who have converted to Jesus as Lord and Savior, and others who consider themselves *followers of Jesus*, but do not call themselves *Christian* due to historical alienation and resistance to indoctrination into western culture. People everywhere may see that through Jesus, God's mercy extends beyond rigid doctrines.

The Holy Spirit and Scripture Bring Enlightenment

This book results from biblical and theological study, as well as the guidance of the Holy Spirit through revelations and thoughts. This text develops a biblical theology for the hope of Christ-mediated salvation for humankind. The term *hope of Christ-mediated salvation for humankind* focuses on Christ's role as Lord and Savior and a faithful biblical understanding that salvation is possible for all, including the eventual salvation of disobedient, half-hearted believers and nonbelievers. Also, salvation is subject to the sovereign will of God.

At the center of salvation is Jesus Christ, the only way to the Father. God desires everyone to be saved. These points are clearly stated in the Bible. Now, if we can understand how the Bible reveals that salvation can be possible for all, then perhaps Christians will believe that the Good News is even better than they could have imagined. Perhaps, the notion of eternal torment as *never-ending* can *end*. Perhaps, all people everywhere will believe that God is good—all the time.

Scripture is inspired, inerrant, and infallible—as written in the original languages of Greek, Hebrew, and Aramaic. Some confusion has been introduced by translations of the Bible. For example, the meaning of the Greek word *aionios*, frequently translated in English as *eternal*, has a significant bearing on understanding biblical truth. Moreover, the Holy Spirit illuminates the meaning of Scripture. If two ideas in the Bible seem inconsistent, Christians may diminish one idea in favor of the other. For example, most churches have determined that everyone will not be saved because of passages like this: "And these will go away into eternal punishment, but the righteous into eternal life" (Matt 25:46 NRSV). However, these churches have dismissed God's stated desire: "God our Savior, who desires everyone to be saved and to come to the knowledge of the truth" (1 Tim 2:3–4 NRSV). Instead of lessening the significance of one of these passages, this book demonstrates how *both* ideas can be true.

Revelations from the Holy Spirit

The book begins by sharing the revelation which came to me on Holy Saturday, April 3, 1999. That revelation prompted me to engage in this study. The Holy Spirit guides believers in the ways of Christ. For God's purposes, the Holy Spirit uses dreams, visions, and other revelations to communicate truth. For example, Jesus said:

> When the Spirit of truth comes, he will guide you into all the truth; for he will not speak on his own, but will speak whatever he hears, and he will declare to you the things that are to come. (John 16:13 NRSV)

Also, the Holy Spirit came on Pentecost, fulfilling the prophecy of Joel:

> In the last days it will be, God declares, that I will pour out my Spirit upon all flesh, and your sons and your daughters shall prophesy, and your young men shall see visions, and your old men shall dream dreams. Even upon my slaves, both men and women, in those days I will pour out my Spirit; and they shall prophesy. And I will show portents in the heaven above and signs on the earth below, blood, and fire, and smoky mist. The sun shall be turned to darkness and the moon to blood, before the coming of the Lord's great and glorious day. Then everyone who calls on the name of the Lord shall be saved. (Acts 2:17–21 NRSV)

Before turning to the matter of prophesy, visions, and dreams, we should note that God declared to *pour out my Spirit upon all flesh,* that is, upon all people—a declaration with universalistic overtones. In addition, we may note that *everyone who calls upon the name of the Lord shall be saved.* We may observe that there is no time limit set by this verse to call upon the Lord. We will later deal with the question of such limits.

The above passage is a clear declaration that the Holy Spirit communicates to people by prophecy, visions and dreams. Many Christians were empowered in this way by the Holy Spirit, as recorded in the New Testament: for example, Stephen's vision of Jesus standing at the right hand of God (Acts 7:55); Peter's vision of a sheet holding many kinds of animals (Acts 10:9–16); Paul's vision of a man of Macedonia pleading for help (Acts 16:9–10); and John's visions in the Book of Revelation. As to whether the Holy Spirit still communicates by revelations, we should observe that the world is still *in the last days* until the Lord returns (Acts 2:17–21). Thus, the biblical proclamation is still in effect.

Dreams, visions, and related revelations from God are not an everyday occurrence for me; nonetheless, they have been significant aspects of my walk with the Lord. The first time I saw a vision was on June 11, 1985. I meditated for nearly ten years on what the Lord was saying through it before writing down its meaning. The second vision came to me on April 2, 1996. Then, several revelations came to me over the next three years. After that, early in the morning on Holy Saturday, April 3, 1999, three visions followed by the new words to the hymn "Beneath the Cross of Jesus" came to me. Then, I received two other revelations that same month, one on April 17 and one on April 19. However, after April 1999, there were no further revelations until November 2, 2012 (that is, *All Souls Day* in Catholicism), which occurred during this research.

I have used the Holy Saturday revelatory song and related revelations to *prompt* study and understanding—that is, studying Scripture for insight. The point of this book is not to prove the occurrence of the revelations, but to describe how the Holy Spirit led me to examine Scripture. Indeed, all valid revelations must be consistent with the Bible. While I believe that revelations from the Holy Spirit help to guide us into truth, I also believe that Scripture contains truth and the two must be consistent. Otherwise, the person has erred in receiving a revelation, or the interpretation of Scripture is in error. Our task as followers of Jesus is to faithfully seek and abide by truth from the Lord. Therefore, this book is not merely about revelations; it is mostly about truth as conveyed by the Word of God with a clear and faithful biblical theology.

The Rest of This Book

The rest of this book looks at Scripture and theological studies while articulating a biblical theology which has existed in the pages of the New Testament since its beginnings, but has been generally overlooked since the sixth century when Augustine's view of everlasting conscious torment became predominant. Chapter 2 describes a dilemma: since Scripture clearly states that God wants to save all people, why does traditional theology hold (by doctrine or by implication) that God does not save all people? Has it missed important points of Scripture? Chapter 3 reviews twelve church fathers on eternal punishment, the doctrine of purgatory including the works of Catherine of Genoa (1447–1510), the traditional descent of Christ into hell, and four prominent twentieth-century theologians. For example, the church fathers' views varied considerably on the subject of eternal punishment—ranging from universal restoration to everlasting conscious torment with no chance of liberation. Gregory of Nyssa held the former view. Augustine held the latter view, which became the predominant view of the church from around the sixth century to today. In chapter 4, a biblical theology resolves the dilemma from chapter 2. God's desire for the salvation of everyone *can* actually occur in accordance with the Bible. In fact, this book presents a more credible resolution than traditional theology with its insistence on endless conscious torment for the lost. Finally, chapter 5 summarizes key points and concludes by urging Christians to stop relying on uncertain interpretations, but instead to adopt the faithful position of trusting Jesus as the one mediator between God and humankind.

2

God Wants All to Be Saved

A Biblical Truth and a Theological Dilemma

CONSIDER BIBLICAL PASSAGES THAT demonstrate God's desire to save everybody. For example,

> God our Savior, who desires everyone to be saved and to come to the knowledge of the truth. (1 Tim 2:3–4 NRSV)

When theological systems are developed and then become part of common thinking, they may acquire an authority of their own—losing sight of basic biblical truths. With this in mind, the passages considered here will aid in understanding the scope of salvation. Since these biblical passages point to salvation for all of humankind, the principles emanating from these passages are noticeably in tension with traditional theology, which holds to some form of everlasting punishment for the lost. Thus, there is a theological dilemma. "Christians today continue to discuss one very old debate—whether some people will end up lost or punished eternally. The dominant view among Orthodox, Catholics, and Protestants has been that all human beings are sinners who deserve to go to hell but that God graciously rescues some—but only some."[1] The question seems settled for most Christians. Yet, what meaning are we Christians to understand from the Scriptures indicating God's desire that everyone be saved? Or that the world has been reconciled to God through Christ? Let us examine some of these passages.

---

1. Placher, *Essentials of Christian Theology*, 334.

Jesus Atoned for the Sins of the World

Atone means to make amends. In the New Testament, atonement was accomplished by Jesus' death on the cross and his resurrection. This divine action is uniquely significant for the eternal destiny of humankind. It is proof of God's desire to save humans, through his one and only Son. Jesus atoned for the sins of humankind, making salvation possible for all who believe in Jesus as Savior and obey Jesus as Lord. There is a threefold understanding in this statement. First, the atonement is intended by God to benefit all humans. Second, a response is required by persons who are able to do so.[2] Third, the fullness of salvation is not simply an assent that Jesus is the Savior; it means that the person fully obeys Jesus as Lord. More will be developed on this point in chapter 4. For now, we want to understand the pivotal role of the atonement.

The work of Jesus Christ, specifically his sacrificial death on the cross, is the atonement that reconciles sinners to God. Since no human being is good enough to save himself or herself from sin and enter eternal life based on his or her own merits, God initiated atonement so that sinners could receive salvation. This was an act of God's great love toward humans.

> For God so loved the world that he gave his only Son, so that everyone who believes in him may not perish but may have eternal life. Indeed, God did not send the Son into the world to condemn the world, but in order that the world might be saved through him. (John 3:16–17 NRSV)

God's love is greater than human sin. Even as God does not tolerate sin, God has provided a way to overcome sin. *The way* is his own Son Jesus Christ:

> Jesus said to him, I am the way, and the truth, and the life. No one comes to the Father except through me. (John 14:6 NRSV)

Jesus is the only way for humans to come to God the Father. Thus, the atonement made by Jesus is essential for the salvation of all human beings.

God intended atonement for all humans. Two passages in 1 John address the atoning sacrifice made by Jesus.

---

2. In this earthly life, certain persons would not be able to respond to God's invitation, which is made possible by Jesus' atonement; such persons could include young children and those who die before birth (whether by abortion or natural causes), as well as the mentally retarded. Persons who never heard about Jesus Christ or the Gospel would not be able to make a response to God's invitation. As this book will show, it is anticipated that the possibility of a response to God's invitation would exist in the afterlife.

The first verse is 1 John 2:2:

> And he [Jesus Christ] is the atoning sacrifice for our sins, and not for ours only but also for the sins of the whole world. (1 John 2:2 NRSV)

It is clear from 1 John 2:2 that the scope of the atonement is universal; that is, Jesus' death and resurrection are intended to benefit all human beings, not just some.

The second verse is 1 John 4:9–10:

> God's love was revealed among us in this way: God sent his only Son into the world so that we might live through him. In this is love, not that we loved God but that he loved us and sent his Son to be the atoning sacrifice for our sins. (1 John 4:9–10 NRSV)

The atonement was God's initiative, an act of love through his Son Jesus Christ, to restore the relationship with humans, who were separated from God because of human sin. This universal atonement, in and of itself, does not mean that all are saved. However, the atonement provides the necessary foundation upon which humans may be saved by God's grace. As we will see later in this chapter, traditional theology presumes that not all humans will be saved. However, there is no solid ground for this presumption. In contrast to traditional theology, the hope of Christ-mediated salvation for all demonstrates how Christ's atonement can benefit all humans through reconciliation and the prospect of eventual salvation.

We can be assured that God desires that *all* persons be saved and has provided the opportunity for *all* to be saved through Jesus Christ. As fully God and fully human, Jesus is uniquely qualified to accomplish the atoning work. For example,

> This is right and is acceptable in the sight of God our Savior, who desires everyone to be saved and to come to the knowledge of the truth. For there is one God; there is also one mediator between God and humankind, Christ Jesus, himself human, who gave himself a ransom for all. (1 Tim 2:3–6 NRSV)

God has the power to accomplish what God desires.

Scripture describes Jesus' atoning work as ransom, substitute, and sacrifice. We will look at each of these purposes and how God uses them to benefit everyone.

Jesus' atonement as a ransom to free captives from sin.

> For the Son of Man came not to be served but to serve, and to give
> his life a ransom for many. (Mark 10:45 NRSV)

First of all, we should not let the word *many* in this verse limit the scope of
people benefited by the atonement; as was just seen above about Jesus "who
gave himself a ransom *for all*" (1 Tim 2:6 NRSV, *emphasis added*). Jesus was
not paying ransom to Satan or to any person. In a sense, Satan does exercise
control over a sinful world and over unredeemed people, even as Jesus referred to Satan as "the ruler of this world" (John 12:31 NRSV). But Satan is
not on the same level as God, and God does not owe Satan anything. Jesus
Christ conquered sin and evil by his death on the cross and resurrection
from the tomb. Thus, by giving his life as a ransom, Jesus attained victory
over all sin and death—freeing humankind from our own sinfulness and
from evil forces opposed to God. Jesus' atonement was necessary only once,
and his victory does not cease upon a person's death. Since Jesus overcame
evil forever, there are no forces of evil to inhibit persons in the afterlife from
accepting God's invitation.

Jesus' atonement as the substitute for us sinners.

All of humankind is in need of the redemptive work of Christ. "All we like
sheep have gone astray; we have all turned to our own way, and the Lord
has laid on him the iniquity of us all" (Isa 53:6 NRSV). Jesus took on our
sins; he substituted for us in our hopeless state. Love is the motivation for
Christ taking our place, as Jesus himself describes his substitution for us.
"No one has greater love than this, to lay down one's life for one's friends"
(John 15:13 NRSV). Indeed, Jesus did lay down his life for us, and furthermore, he substituted for us in a way that no one else could ever do:

> that is, in Christ God was reconciling the world to himself, not
> counting their trespasses against them, and entrusting the mes-
> sage of reconciliation to us. So we are ambassadors for Christ,
> since God is making his appeal through us; we entreat you on
> behalf of Christ, be reconciled to God. For our sake he made him
> to be sin who knew no sin, so that in him we might become the
> righteousness of God." (2 Cor 5:19–21 NRSV)

Therefore, in Christ, God was reconciling the world to himself and not counting their sins against them. Those who have been reconciled to God are to spread the message of reconciliation. As a result of Jesus becoming sin for us, that is, becoming our *substitute*, we are no longer bound to a continuing existence of sinfulness and its consequences. Since God no longer counts the world's sins against them, it is clear that God has already reconciled the world to himself. It would seem best to think that God can continue the reconciliation process which God started, rather than reverting to traditional theology thinking that God would accept an *unreconciled* state.

Jesus' atonement as the atoning sacrifice for human sin.

According to the pattern of sacrifice established by God in the Old Testament, animal blood sacrifices were made by the Hebrew people to atone for their sins. Lambs were a common sacrifice, although other animals were also used in the sacrificial system. John the Baptist said about Jesus, "Here is the Lamb of God who takes away the sin of the world!" (John 1:29 NRSV). The Baptizer's statement is universal: "the sin of the world." Lambs were specifically associated with the Passover, at which time in Israel's history, God brought about the deliverance of his people from bondage in Egypt. Jesus ate the Passover meal with his disciples on the night in which he was betrayed, gave himself over to the authorities, was falsely tried and then crucified. He is called the Passover Lamb. "For Christ, our Passover lamb, has been sacrificed" (1 Cor 5:7 New International Version).

The Day of Atonement, described in Leviticus 16, was the annual day of ritual to atone for the sins of the priest and of the people of Israel. On this occasion, a bull, two rams, and two goats were used for the ritual. A young bull was sacrificed for the sins of the high priest and his household. The two rams were burnt offerings. The two goats were used for atonement for the people's sins. One goat was sacrificed and the high priest sprinkled its blood on the atonement cover of the Ark of the Covenant, inside the Holy of Holies. Then, the high priest laid his hands on the head of the live goat and confessed all of the sins of the people on the goat, which is called the *scapegoat*. The goat was then led into the wilderness, carrying away the people's sins. It is to be noted that on the Day of Atonement, all the people's sins were removed—but the ritual had to be repeated each year. Jesus' sacrifice is the atonement that lasts forever.

Jesus' sinless life and sacrificial death fulfilled the law. As the Son of God, Jesus accomplished what no fallen human could. Through the atonement, Christ reconciled *the world* or *all people* to God; ransomed all humans who were captive to sin; became the substitute for our sin; and fulfilled the atoning sacrifice for sin. Jesus' atonement shows purposeful action to make salvation available for all. With this understanding of universal atonement, God's desire that everyone be saved is biblical truth which must be reflected in theological thought. Although the circumstances of life vary and saving faith for every person may be beyond our collective vision, God has a plan and the power to accomplish what God intends. We may remember Jesus' words to his disciples, who asked, "'Then who can be saved?' But Jesus looked at them and said, 'For mortals it is impossible, but for God all things are possible'" (Matt 19:25–26 NRSV).

Theological views of salvation and the atonement.

The prominent Protestant views of salvation are Calvinism and Arminianism. The former is based on particular atonement—limited to those persons who receive salvation—and God's unconditional election of the persons who are to be saved, that is, *predestination*. On the other hand, Arminianism is based on universal atonement, in which Christ died for the atonement of all people, and salvation occurs for those who believe in Jesus as their Lord and Savior. Calvinism stresses the sovereignty of God in making salvation decisions; Arminianism places the ability on each human to make a salvation decision because God has provided grace to enable such a decision. We have already seen that God "desires everyone to be saved" (1 Tim 2:4 NRSV). To be valid, theological views must take into account God's express purposes. Calvinism is a theological system with dreadful results: people who have never even heard of Jesus Christ or the gospel may face eternal damnation. One has to wonder why people would even be born as creations of God, only to experience a dismal eternal existence. Under Arminianism, human freewill limits God's sovereignty—God cannot save everyone as he wants. The two theological systems seem seriously flawed, yet each has some merit. Neither system has reconciled the apparent dilemma of whether God's sovereignty and human freewill can co-exist. The hope of Christ-mediated salvation for all puts to rest the problems of the prevailing theological systems. More importantly, it reflects the will of God—that all people be saved—as expressed in the Bible.

More Passages Demonstrating
God's Desire That All Be Saved

Some of the passages in this section may be unfamiliar to the casual reader of the Bible. They may be infrequently preached as the subject of Sunday sermons. They may be overlooked in many a Bible study by individuals and groups. Still, these passages are included in the inspired Word of God, and therefore, their meaning must be faithfully considered. These biblical passages provide more evidence that God desires everyone to be saved and indications that all can be saved under God's plan as revealed in the Bible. These passages provide some of the basis for the biblical theology for the hope of Christ-mediated salvation for all that is developed in chapter 4.

All people will see the salvation of God.

Before Jesus began his earthly ministry, John the Baptist prepared the way, calling the people to repent. Luke 3:4–6 refers to Isaiah 40:3–5. Isaiah's prophecy crescendos with this marvelous promise:

> Then the glory of the Lord shall be revealed, and all people shall see it together, for the mouth of the Lord has spoken. (Isa 40:5 NRSV)

The first phase of Isaiah's prophecy was accomplished in the sixth century BC when all the nations around Israel witnessed the return of the Jews to their land. There, they would rebuild the Temple and worship the God of Abraham, Isaac and Jacob. Still, there is much more to Isaiah's prophecy. All four Gospels in the New Testament connect John the Baptist to the prophecy of Isaiah as *a voice of one calling in the wilderness.* The Baptizer called people to repentance and baptism in order to *prepare the way of the Lord.* As such, John was announcing the coming of Jesus, the Messiah. The *glory of the Lord* has been revealed in Jesus Christ; thus, the passage in Luke speaks of salvation sent by God, "and all flesh shall see the salvation of God" (Luke 3:6 NRSV). Through the centuries, many have seen the salvation of God through the Lord and Savior Jesus Christ. On the other hand, many people have not even had the opportunity to hear of Jesus. This prophecy will be consummated by Jesus in the age to come when all people will see the salvation of God. Thus, this biblical text enhances our understanding of God's plan to restore humanity, just as God brought the people of Israel back to the Promised Land from exile.

Jesus will draw all people to himself.

Jesus predicted his death on the cross, saying:

> "And I, when I am lifted up from the earth, will draw all people to myself." He said this to indicate the kind of death he was to die. (John 12:32–33 NRSV)

Jesus' statement was made in the context of the Son of Man being glorified (John 12:23), the Father being glorified (John 12:28), and judgment of the world and driving out the ruler of this world (John 12:31). Thus, Jesus' death on the cross will result in these outcomes. Drawing all people to Jesus is not incompatible with any of these purposes. In fact, when judgment is put in its proper perspective of correction and renewal (as amplified later in this chapter), it can be seen that Jesus' death on the cross will indeed draw all people to himself—for the glory of God, for justice and righteousness, for eliminating evil, and for salvation. Thus, this passage implies a universal attraction to Jesus Christ and to salvation through him.

Jesus tasted death for everyone.

> But we do see Jesus, who for a little while was made lower than the angels, now crowned with glory and honor because of the suffering of death, so that by the grace of God he might taste death for everyone. It was fitting that God, for whom and through whom all things exist, in bringing many children to glory, should make the pioneer of their salvation perfect through sufferings. (Heb 2:9–10 NRSV)

According to the text, Jesus experienced suffering and death for *everyone*. Moreover, the text specifies that all things exist for God and through God. This gives added weight to the idea that Jesus died for everyone. By saying "many children," a large unspecified number, the text does not need to be interpreted that some are left out; that is, that not all are ultimately saved. "Everyone" and "all things" have already been stated. Thus, this passage sheds light on God's plan for all to be saved.

God refocuses human disobedience into mercy for all.

> Just as you were once disobedient to God but have now received mercy because of their disobedience, so they have now been

disobedient in order that, by the mercy shown to you, they too may now receive mercy. For God has imprisoned all in disobedience so that he may be merciful to all. (Rom 11:30–32 NRSV)

The context is God's treatment of Israel considering that not all Jews believed in Jesus as Messiah. This does not mean that Israel was no longer God's chosen people. In fact, God brought Gentiles to salvation, grafted in with Israel (Rom 11:17). Then, Paul gives a warning and further explanation: "So that you may not claim to be wiser than you are, brothers and sisters, I want you to understand this mystery: a hardening has come upon part of Israel, until the full number of the Gentiles has come in. And so all Israel will be saved" (Rom 11:25–26 NRSV). We cannot assume, by this text, what the full number of Gentiles is. What is clear is that the principle at the end of this passage is effective not only for Israel but also for Gentiles: God has kept everyone in disobedience so that he may have mercy on all (Rom 11:32). This speaks of God's authority and also of God's intention to show mercy to all people.

Jesus' act of righteousness leads to life for all persons.

Therefore just as one man's trespass led to condemnation for all, so one man's act of righteousness leads to justification and life for all. For just as by the one man's disobedience the many were made sinners, so by the one man's obedience the many will be made righteous. (Rom 5:18–19 NRSV)

Here we come across the use of "all" in 5:18 and "many" in 5:19. Considering just verse 18, it is clear that one man's (Adam's) trespass led to condemnation for all persons, and one man's (Jesus Christ's) act of righteousness leads to justification for all. Considering verse 19, "many" may simply be used as a contrast with "one man." There is no concrete reason to believe that the use of "many" limits the number ("all") who are justified and receive life as a result of Jesus' action. Instead, the use of "many" is probably best thought to clarify that the "one man" used twice in each verse is not included in "all," as explained by Thomas Talbott:

It seems to me indisputable, therefore, that Paul had in mind one group of individuals—"the many," which includes all human beings except for the first and the second Adam—and he envisioned that each of the two Adams stands in the same relationship to that one group of individuals. The first Adam's act of disobedience brought doom upon them all, but the second Adam's act of obedience undid the doom and eventually brings justification and life to them all.[3]

The "second Adam" is Jesus Christ whose redeeming work leads to life for all persons. In essence, Jesus has reversed the effect of Adam's sin, making salvation possible for all. This passage demonstrates that God's plan for all to be saved is moving forward.

All will be made alive in Christ.

> For since death came through a human being, the resurrection of the dead has also come through a human being; for as all die in Adam, so all will be made alive in Christ. But each in his own order: Christ the first fruits, then at his coming those who belong to Christ. Then comes the end, when he hands over the kingdom to God the Father, after he has destroyed every ruler and every authority and power. For he must reign until he has put all his enemies under his feet. (1 Cor 15:21–25 NRSV)

This passage makes a similar point to that in Romans 5:18–19. Death came through Adam, but life comes through Christ—for all. Being made alive has an interesting sequence: first is Christ who is referred to as *the first fruits*, then at Christ's coming those who belong to him, then the kingdom which could include all others. In fact, the biblical theology for the hope of Christ-mediated salvation for all developed in chapter 4 corresponds with the two groups: that is, those who obey Christ during earthly life and those who later enter the kingdom loyal to Christ. Then, Christ hands over the kingdom to God the Father, but not until he has destroyed opposing powers. This *Christ-mediated* process—from enduring the cross to destroying powers opposed to his mission to handing over the kingdom to the Father—suggests a kingdom that is complete and likewise universal because "all will be made alive in Christ" (1 Cor 15:22 NRSV).

God is all in all.

> Then comes the end, when he hands over the kingdom to God the Father, after he has destroyed every ruler and every authority and

3. Talbott, *The Inescapable Love of God*, 57.

power. For he must reign until he has put all his enemies under his feet. The last enemy to be destroyed is death. For "God has put all things in subjection under his feet." But when it says, "All things are put in subjection," it is plain that this does not include the one who put all things in subjection under him. When all things are subjected to him, then the Son himself will also be subjected to the one who put all things in subjection under him, so that God may be all in all. (1 Cor 15:24–28 NRSV)

Continuing from the previous paragraph (with verses 24 and 25 overlapping for context), the verses in this section inform us that Christ will destroy all opposing powers before handing the kingdom over to God the Father. God has put *all things* under Christ's feet, an action which indicates the divine intention to restore the creative purpose in Christ, whereby "all things have been created through him and for him" (Col 1:16 NRSV). Christ will reign until he has put all his enemies under his feet. Enemies are forces, including satanic powers, that oppose Christ's mission of establishing God's kingdom. Humans are not enemies of God because through Christ God was reconciling the world to himself (2 Cor 5:19), and through Christ God was pleased to reconcile all things to himself (Col 1:20). Still, humans who do not obey Jesus as Lord may need purification with accompanying repentance in the afterlife. The last enemy that Christ will destroy is death, thus paving the way for new life. Therefore, when *all things* become subjected to Christ, then God is all in all. This passage was a key to Origen's theology for the restoration of all things, which we will examine in the next chapter. This passage portrays a glorious conclusion whereby *all things* (including all people) are under the authority of Christ and consequently of God

God brings salvation to all people.

For the grace of God has appeared, bringing salvation to all, training us to renounce impiety and worldly passions, and in the present age to live lives that are self-controlled, upright, and godly, while we wait for the blessed hope and the manifestation of the glory of our great God and Savior, Jesus Christ. (Titus 2:11–13 NRSV)

The context leading up to this passage is Paul's instructions to Titus on teaching older men, older women, young men, and slaves. That the grace of God brings salvation to these groups and to all people demonstrates that God intends for salvation to come about. The grace of God brings salvation to all (2:11). Then, the text reflects the fruit that should result from salvation "in the present age." Indeed, when people receive salvation, their lives are changed and they bear much fruit for God. These present fruit of salvation do not negate the grace of God bringing salvation to those in the age to come. In fact, in chapter 4 we will examine the distinction between those who obey Christ and thus bear fruit versus those whose allegiance to Christ is lacking.

All things reconciled through Christ to God.

> For in him [the Son] all the fullness of God was pleased to dwell, and through him God was pleased to reconcile to himself all things, whether on earth or in heaven, by making peace through the blood of his cross. (Col 1:19–20 NRSV)

The reconciliation and peace brought about through the Son of God is clearly a divine initiative, not a human one. It is noteworthy that *all things* include *all humans* and much more. "There is also a *cosmic* dimension, in that Christ has not merely reconciled individual people with God but has set in motion a much larger, all-encompassing peace (Col 1:20)."[4] The reconciliation described in this passage has been accomplished, while the end result of God's plan is a total restoration of creation.

All things gathered up in Christ.

> With all wisdom and insight he has made known to us the mystery of his will, according to his good pleasure that he set forth in Christ, as a plan for the fullness of time, to gather up all things in him, things in heaven and things on earth. (Eph 1:8–10 NRSV)

As in Colossians 1:19–20, we see that God's will is to gather up ("bring . . . together" NIV) all things. Referencing both of the passages, Brenda B. Colijn observes: "Although reconciliation in the New Testament is generally concerned with human beings, God's reconciliation of all things (*ta panta*) in Christ suggests that God's purposes reach beyond human beings to embrace the rest of fractured creation."[5] Such an observation serves to confirm that God's purposes for reconciliation and unification are beyond human

---

4. DeSilva, *An Introduction to the New Testament*, 695.

5. Colijn, *Images of Salvation in the New Testament*, 191.

understanding. Even so, we Christians should accept reconciliation as God's purpose, not dismissing the idea that *God wants all to be saved.*

The world is reconciled to God.

Through Christ, God has reconciled the world to himself. Furthermore, God does not count people's trespasses against them.

> For the love of Christ urges us on, because we are convinced that one has died for all; therefore all have died. And he died for all, so that those who live might live no longer for themselves, but for him who died and was raised for them. From now on, therefore, we regard no one from a human point of view; even though we once knew Christ from a human point of view, we know him no longer in that way. So if anyone is in Christ, there is a new creation: everything old has passed away; see, everything has become new! All this is from God, who reconciled us to himself through Christ, and has given us the ministry of reconciliation; that is, in Christ God was reconciling the world to himself, not counting their trespasses against them, and entrusting the message of reconciliation to us. (2 Cor 5:14–19 NRSV)

This passage indicates that Christ died for all. The purpose is that those who live do so for Christ. It is apparent that this goal is yet not reached. Nevertheless, we are not to view people from a human point of view. If anyone is in Christ, there is a new creation, and there is no limitation imposed when this must occur; that is, a new creation can occur whenever someone is in Christ. All of this is set in the context that in Christ God has reconciled the world to himself—a divine initiative to be in relationship with humankind. Moreover, the reconciliation has been accomplished, as provided by God through Christ.

Out of destruction, God will bring a new beginning.

"But by the same word the present heavens and earth have been reserved for fire, being kept until the Day of Judgment and destruction of the godless" (2 Pet 3:7 NRSV). In the days of Noah, God flooded the world, destroying the wicked while saving Noah and his family. The final destruction of the entire world will be by fire. However, this is no ordinary fire, for "the earth and everything that is done on it will be disclosed" (2 Pet 3:10 NRSV). This fire apparently will reveal human actions, purify people, and usher in righteousness where there is sin and wrongdoing. "But, in accordance with his [God's] promise, we wait for new heavens and a new earth, where righteousness is at home" (2 Pet 3:13 NRSV). The fire is used by God to prepare new heavens and a new earth filled with righteousness. Since followers of Christ already have the righteousness of Christ and the new earth will be inhabited only by the redeemed, the new earth will be ready after it has been purified (Rom 8:18–23). God apparently wants more people for the new earth. In fact, God has great patience so that all may repent. "The Lord is not slow about his promise, as some think of slowness, but is patient with you, not wanting any to perish, but all to come to repentance" (2 Pet 3:9 NRSV). God is patient because he does not want any to perish— an indication of God's intention. While waiting, we are to live holy lives, recognizing that God's patience results in salvation for Christians and for others. "Therefore, beloved, while you are waiting for these things, strive to be found by him at peace, without spot or blemish; and regard the patience of our Lord as salvation" (2 Pet 3:14–15 NRSV).

Death and Hades will give up the dead in them.

> And the sea gave up the dead that were in it, Death and Hades gave up the dead that were in them, and all were judged according to what they had done. Then Death and Hades were thrown into the lake of fire. This is the second death, the lake of fire. (Rev 20:13–14 NRSV)

Since Death and Hades will no longer hold any dead people, what is the second death? It is the lake of fire, but how do the lost experience the second death there? Traditional theology has assumed that the *doctrine* of endless conscious torment is confirmed by the second death. However, if that were the case, the second death would not be death at all. The second death in this context is that Death itself is dead. Already, because of Christ's death and resurrection, those who are in Christ have been freed from the power of death. "There is therefore now no condemnation for those who are in Christ Jesus. For the law of the Spirit of life in Christ Jesus has set you free from the law of sin and of death" (Rom 8:1–2 NRSV). Thus, the purpose of Death and Hades being thrown into the lake of fire is to burn up these two intrusions which were never intended from the beginning, while purifying humans who are not in Christ so that they may live with God forever. This point is specifically brought out by this passage: "But as for the cowardly, the faithless, the polluted, the murderers, the fornicators, the sorcerers, the idolaters, and all liars, their place will be in the lake that burns with fire and sulfur, which is the second death" (Rev 21:8 NRSV). Under the hope of Christ-mediated salvation for all, the second death happens in the lake of fire when the person who had died physically apart from Christ now dies in a spiritual sense and is born again by the love of God, the redemption of Jesus Christ, and the power of the Holy Spirit. The person's repentance and purification complete this process—the same as repentance and sanctification bring people in this life to the fullness of salvation. Emptying Death and Hades of the dead and restoring persons after the second death demonstrates that the framework for the hope of Christ-mediated salvation for all is in place by God's plan.

Jesus Christ is Lord of all.

> Therefore God also highly exalted him and gave him the name that is above every name, so that at the name of Jesus every knee should bend, in heaven and on earth and under the earth, and every tongue should confess that Jesus Christ is Lord, to the glory of God the Father. (Phil 2:9–11 NRSV)

What is striking about this passage is that every human being from all times, as well as other beings such as angels delineated by "in heaven and on earth and under the earth" will confess Jesus as Lord. That Jesus will be confessed as Lord by every element of humanity should cause everyone to marvel at the scope of His Lordship. Moreover, by referring to every knee and every tongue, the passage suggests that every person will be present with Jesus. The word *confess* is key to understanding the passage. It appears that the word's meaning has been stretched by traditional theology to fit its perspective. More will be said on this point and the application of the passage in the next section. Suffice it to say for now that this passage points to the hope of Christ-mediated salvation for all.

An Example of Divergent Theological Thinking

The previous paragraph reviewed Philippians 2:9–11 (NRSV): "Therefore God also highly exalted him and gave him the name that is above every name, so that at the name of Jesus every knee should bend, in heaven and on earth and under the earth, and every tongue should confess that Jesus Christ is Lord, to the glory of God the Father." It seems to be an obvious passage supporting hope of salvation for all. Yet, the passage is the subject of controversy. Traditional theology holds that some people will confess that Jesus is Lord against their will. Thus, the passage illustrates how the theological debate continues as to whether God's desire for all to be saved will be accomplished.

The Philippians passage is an echo of Isaiah: "By myself I have sworn, from my mouth has gone forth in righteousness a word that shall not return: 'To me every knee shall bow, every tongue shall swear'" (Isa 45:23 NRSV). The prophecy of Isaiah did not cease, but is expanded in Philippians to include all beings with apt awareness expressing their loyalty. "The prophet had expected a turning to Yahweh of all the nations upon earth. The hymn (Phil 2:5–11) extends the scope to include all sentient beings throughout the cosmos."[6] The Philippians passage specifically applies the Isaiah prophecy to Jesus. Thus, Jesus has not only fulfilled the Old Testament prophecy, he has become Lord of all. Every knee shall bow and every tongue *confess* that Jesus is Lord.

The word *confess* in 2:11 is subject to interpretation. It is "taken to denote either 'admit and acknowledge' or 'confess with thanksgiving.' While it is true that the Septuagint typically employs the term of the confession of praise and thanksgiving, it can occasionally be used of acknowledging something against one's will. . . ."[7] Let us view the possible range of meanings starting with the most purposeful to the least commonly used:

1. If the word means *confess with thanksgiving*, every person making such a declaration has already been united with Jesus as Lord and Savior.

2. If the word means *admit and acknowledge*, every person will acknowledge Jesus as Lord; to acknowledge is a step on the way to confessing with thanksgiving.

3. If the word means *acknowledging something against one's will*, it does not mean that such people will not be saved ultimately; it means that they have not accepted salvation yet. It should be remembered that the purpose of this biblical text is to emphasize that Jesus is Lord of all—*in heaven and on earth and under the earth.*

The third meaning is often cited by those who hold to the traditional theology of endless conscious punishment for the lost. Traditional theology

6. Martin, *A Hymn of Christ*, 256.
7. Bockmuehl, *The Epistle to the Philippians*, 1998, 146–7.

seems to want to start with the theological view, and then locate a biblical understanding within its theological framework. However, it should be remembered that the third meaning was used only occasionally, as noted above. In addition, there is no "timeframe" specified for the accomplishment of this passage. It may not be a static picture; instead, it may be fluid in application. Finally, the plain reading of the passage calls for the meaning of the word *confess* to be the same for all people, not differentiated by groups of people. Thus, it is best to accept this passage as evidence that ultimately everyone will thankfully give allegiance to Jesus as Lord.

There is an apparent universal purpose behind this text. Compare this to Ephesians 1:10: "It was in order that every created being in heaven, on earth and under the earth might ultimately be reconciled to God by voluntarily and joyfully pledging allegiance to the one who chose the lowly path of self-effacement and of humble service to others."[8] Thus, Philippians 2:9–11 supports an expansive view of the scope of salvation, as well as a heightened sense of the significance of serving our Lord Jesus Christ.

With such a magnanimous Lord, the only acceptable response is total allegiance to Christ—from first-century Christians living in the Roman Empire to twenty-first century Christians living in current cultures. Following Jesus as Lord requires our all—from each of us. We will return to the importance of obeying Jesus as Lord in chapter 4.

Presumed Limits on Christ-Mediated Salvation for All

At this point, we have viewed biblical evidence which supports the biblical truth that God wants to save everyone, and we have seen an example of how interpretations of a biblical passage can affect the understanding of the broader biblical truth. We will now examine some of the presuppositions which have served as artificial constraints. While there are biblical requirements for persons to be saved, there are also a number of invalid theological limits which have been imposed over the centuries. As will be seen in the next chapter, one such limit is the idea that the lost will suffer endless punishment or torment. This idea was supported by Augustine in the fifth century and has been the prevalent view since around the sixth century. In this section, we will examine views which can be characterized as *traditional theology* because they represent ideas such as endless punishment that have been passed down for centuries largely unchallenged.

8. Hawthorne and Martin, *Philippians*, 129.

Presumption that eternal punishment is endless or everlasting.

"And these will go away into eternal punishment, but the righteous into eternal life" (Matt 25:46 NRSV). The Greek word *aionios* is translated *eternal* for both eternal punishment and eternal life.[9] Some contend that since the same Greek word appears twice in the same text, eternal punishment must mean everlasting in order for eternal life to also mean everlasting. However, the meaning of *aionios* is more complex than that.

To grasp this complexity, we turn to two authoritative sources. First, Ramelli and Konstan recently researched the terms *aionios* and *aidios*.[10] Their findings in regard to *aionios* confirm its complexity and wide range of meaning. One meaning of *aionios* is that it can refer to a long period of time or an age, particularly the age to come.

> The term *aionios*, which seems to have been introduced by Plato and comes into its own in the Scriptures, is more complex [than *aidios*]: it may indicate a long period of time, or, in the Platoniz-ing writers, an atemporal or transcendental timelessness. Very broadly, *aionios* corresponds to the uses of *aion*, which means a lifetime, a generation, or an entire age or epoch, particularly in Stoicizing contexts; in Christian writings, *aion* may refer to the temporal age prior to creation, to the present world, or, most often, to the epoch to come in the next world. *Aionios* may also acquire the connotation of strict eternity, particularly when it is applied to God or divine things: here, the sense of the adjective is conditioned by the subject it modifies. There is also a technical sense in Christian theology, in which *aionios* may refer more specifically to the *aion* that follows upon the resurrection but precedes the final reintegration or apocatastasis, which in the view of Origen and his followers will signal the salvation of all, including those who have until this moment been subject to redemptive punishment. With the apocatastasis, all time, and hence all *aiones*, come to an end.[11]

At this point, we may wonder why such a complex word has been interpreted with a rigid meaning by traditional theology, which does not take into account that *aionios* can refer to a long period of time or an age, particularly

9. A major source of confusion on this issue is that the translation of *aionios* in the King James Version is *everlasting* when used with punishment and *eternal* when used with life. Thus, it reads: "And these shall go away into everlasting punishment: but the righteous into life eternal" (Matt 25:46 KJV).

10. Ramelli and Konstan, *Terms for Eternity*.

11. Ibid, 237.

the age to come. "In particular, when it [*aionios*] is associated with life or punishment, in the Bible and in Christian authors who keep themselves close to the Biblical usage, it denotes their belonging to the world to come."[12] Therefore, with the meaning of *aionios* as the age to come, punishment for each of the lost could occur in the age to come, and all of those purified and restored could be part of the blissful kingdom of God.

For additional understanding of the meaning of *aionios* in the context we are probing, let us turn to another scholar on this subject. Jürgen Moltmann has delved deeply into the meaning of *aionios* applicable to the context in which this study is exploring.

> The Greek word *aionios*, like the Hebrew word *olam*, means time without a fixed end, a long time, but not time that is 'eternal' in the absolute, timeless sense of Greek metaphysics. Consequently there are plurals *olamim* or *aiones*, which there cannot be for timeless eternity, because timeless eternity exists only in the singular. If damnation and the torments of hell are 'eternal,' they are then *aeonic*, long-lasting, or End-time states. Only God himself is 'eternal' in the absolute sense, and 'unending' in the qualitative sense.[13]

Thus, *aionios* can be an age or eon, the duration of which is indefinite. The two uses of *aionios*, both translated as *eternal* in Matthew 25:46, can allow for eternal punishment in its eon and eternal life in its eon. Even so, the person experiencing eternal punishment or correction would not know if and when it would end. The age of eternal life would not end just because the age of eternal punishment ends. Eternal life could continue forever.

Presumption that there is no opportunity for salvation after death.

One of the rationales for traditional theology is that humans live once and then face judgment. "And just as it is appointed for mortals to die once, and after that the judgment. . . ." (Heb 9:27 NRSV). However, what is meant by *judgment*? Traditional theology assumes that judgment is punitive, endless, and even everlasting conscious torment. Another way to understand judgment is that it is corrective and restorative. This understanding of judgment fulfills God's desire that everyone be saved. "God is too pure (read 'too loving') to allow evil of any kind to survive forever in his creation. He will

12. Ibid, 238.

13. Moltmann, *The Coming of God*, 242.

not, therefore, merely quarantine the evil in hell, but will instead destroy it altogether even as he regenerates the evil ones themselves."[14] With such an understanding, judgment takes on a new meaning. The punishment resulting from it sounds more like pruning, which Christians experience during their earthly walk toward obedience with Christ, than the never-ending punishment of traditional theology. As a caveat, nothing in this paper should be construed that waiting for possible salvation in the afterlife is a good notion; likewise, for the marginal Christian, postponing a decision to trust and obey Christ during this life is a bad idea.[15] To resume the Scripture from above, "so Christ, having been offered once to bear the sins of many, will appear a second time, not to deal with sin, but to save those who are eagerly waiting for him" (Heb 9:28 NRSV). It is incomparably better to be *among those eagerly waiting for him* than to be among those desperately waiting for a savior while undergoing eternal punishment.

Presumption that there is no opportunity for repentance after death.

This issue is similar to the previous one. Some who hold the traditional view may add that the lost person is so hardened that he or she would not make a choice to love God and be aligned with Christ. Nonetheless, turning away from sin and toward God would be a natural step after eternal punishment, correction, and restoration. There is no scriptural prohibition against repentance after death. In fact, descriptions of eternal punishment such as "eternal fire," "lake of fire," "weeping and gnashing of teeth," and "the worm that never dies" imply repentance as the outcome of eternal punishment and correction.

> Jesus often warned his audience about the coming judgment in very striking terms. He spoke of fire (Matt 5:22; 18:8, 9, 45, 47), of "eternal fire" (Matt 18:45, 47; 25:41), an unquenched fire that would not go out (Mark 9:48) accompanied by worms that will not die (Mark 9:48). Jesus refers to the place where the fire burns as Gehenna (Matt 23:33). It is a place of judgment (Matt 12:41–42), condemnation (Matt 23:33), 'eternal punishment' (Matt 25:46), and divine wrath (Matt 3:7, 12; Luke 3:7, 17). Sometimes Jesus spoke in the imagery of expulsion to "outer darkness," where there

14. Talbott, "Christ Victorious," 28.

15. For more discussion of these points, see the chapter 5 section "Steps That Christians Can Take from Here."

will be weeping and gnashing of teeth (Matt 8:12; 22:13; 25:30; 24:51). The diversity of the images that, if taken literally, would be somewhat contradictory (flames and outer darkness) alerts us to the metaphorical nature of the language employed here.[16]

Therefore, *fire* could be a metaphor for purification, *weeping and gnashing of teeth* could indicate heart-felt remorse and repentance, and *the worm that never dies* could signify continued life. Repentance is necessary for salvation. Whereas the above biblical images are used by traditional theology to demonstrate conscious endless punishment, they may actually signal something much different: an opportunity for repentance after death.

Pause for reflection.

We will consider more presumptions made by traditional theology later in this chapter, but already it can be seen that traditional theology has made assumptions which have skewed the results. It is no wonder that the theological debate continues. The hope of Christ-mediated salvation for all explains how the biblical truth that God wants all to be saved can actually happen. Next we will look at a branch of traditional theology which has created a presumption by adding restrictions to Scripture.

A theology that adds restrictions to the Bible.

A restrictivist view of salvation, or *restrictivism*, is "the belief that Jesus Christ is the only Savior for all humanity and that it is not possible to attain salvation apart from explicit knowledge of Jesus Christ."[17] Therefore, under this view, in order to receive salvation, a person must explicitly know of Jesus Christ and believe in Jesus Christ as Savior. Further, belief in Jesus Christ must come before the person's death. The striking element of this view is that if a person has never even heard about Jesus Christ, and therefore has no opportunity to believe in Jesus as Savior, that person receives eternal damnation without any hope of redemption. The strength of restrictivism is its emphasis on the uniqueness of Jesus Christ as the Savior. Salvation comes from Christ and no other. However, its weaknesses include defining, by default, the eternal destiny of those who have no opportunity to hear about Jesus Christ in their lifetimes. A significant improvement to

16. MacDonald, *The Evangelical Universalist*, 142.

17. Boyd and Eddy, *Across the Spectrum*, 271.

restrictivism would be to explicitly state that the eternal destiny of the un-evangelized is unknown. The Bible informs us about how persons become saved, but it does not explicitly tell us who will not be saved. As a result of the presumption of the restrictivist view, some see God as unfair. Restrictivist Carl F. H. Henry argues against this. "The justice of God is questioned also by some critics who protest that election-love is discriminatory and therefore a violation of justice. But all love is preferential or it would not be love."[18] Henry's comparison of God's *election-love* to human preferential love is mystifying. Milliard Erickson refers to restrictivism as "the traditional exclusivist approach"[19] or "The Orthodox View."[20] The problem with these designations is that they seem to imply that restrictivism is the established view of Christianity. However, there is definite disagreement with this notion. "From the early church fathers to the present day, Christians have not come to one mind on the fate of those who die never hearing the gospel of Jesus Christ."[21]

Theological errors.

Theological thought can err in many ways. As we have just seen, restrictivism adds a devastating constraint to salvation, withholding even the possibility of salvation from all who have never heard of Jesus Christ. Imagine the billions of people throughout the world and throughout the centuries who have never heard the gospel! Are we to believe that they are damned forever? Earlier in this chapter, we saw that certain theological thinking has presumed the meaning of eternal punishment to be endless conscious torment. This creates an erroneous view of God as unreasonable, uncaring, and distant. Although these characterizations do not accurately reflect God, they may keep some people from wanting to know God. Theological views can also err by eliminating biblical requirements for salvation. Some would mistakenly remove Jesus Christ from his essential role in salvation, even grievously substituting pluralism for the unique saving work of Christ. With all of the conflicting theological views, it may be difficult to discern the truth of Scripture. The value of the hope of Christ-mediated salvation for all is that it upholds biblical standards, while correcting theological errors

18. Henry, "Is It Fair?" 253–254.

19. Erickson, "The Fate of Those Who Never Hear," 12.

20. Erickson, "The State of the Question," 23.

21. Sanders, "Introduction," 15–16.

which have hampered the view of salvation. Furthermore, to understand God's purposes for salvation, we must know God and understand the *heart* of God. The Bible gives valuable perspectives about God and God's relationship with people. An important question to ask when considering any theological work is this: does it truly reflect God as revealed in Scripture?

The Heart of God

Confidence in God's intention to save everyone may come down to how we understand the character of God—or the *heart* of God. There is much in Scripture telling us about God. Again, over the centuries there has been a wide variety of theological thoughts, some of which have led to erroneous ideas that are still prevalent today.

God is Love.

> So we have known and believe the love that God has for us. God is love, and those who abide in love abide in God, and God abides in them. (1 John 4:16 NRSV)

This verse tells us that God loves us and also that *God is Love*. Therefore, the nature or heart of God is love. Jürgen Moltmann puts it this way: "For God it is axiomatic to love, for he cannot deny himself. For God it is axiomatic to love freely, for he is God. There is consequently no reason why we should not understand God as being from eternity self-communicating love. This does not make him 'his own prisoner.' It means that he remains true to himself."[22] The effect for humans is that God will always be love, and God will always love us. "O give thanks to the Lord, for he is good; his steadfast love endures forever!" (Ps 118:1, 29 NRSV). There is no contradiction between the love of God and the wrath of God. Also, there is no contradiction between God's love and justice. God's wrath and justice, both of which have been misconstrued by traditional theology, will be addressed below.

---

22. Moltmann, *The Trinity and the Kingdom of God*, 107–8.

The mercy of God.

The Bible is full of instances of God showing mercy—either to individuals or groups of people. God gives mercy when God determines it best; it is not according to our timetables for ourselves or others.

> The Lord is merciful and gracious, slow to anger and abounding in steadfast love. He will not always accuse, nor will he keep his anger forever. He does not deal with us according to our sins, nor repay us according to our iniquities. (Ps 103:8–10 NRSV)

The Lord understands the human condition and knows our sinful behavior. Still, God continues to have mercy on us. Two immeasurable distances are used in the psalm for illustrations.

> For as the heavens are high above the earth, so great is his steadfast love toward those who fear him; as far as the east is from the west, so far he removes our transgressions from us. (Ps 103:11–12 NRSV)

God's love for us is beyond our understanding, even though we can feel God's love inside us. In Psalm 103, we notice that God's love is focused on those who *fear him*. God's love is not limited to a few; God loves the whole world (John 3:16). Yet, God has a relationship with those who love, trust, and reverence him. For the Lord to remove our sin *as far as the east is from the west* is a promise of boundless worth. The removed sin will never be held against us. There are no boundaries on God's love and mercy.

The faithfulness of Christ.

> The saying is sure: If we have died with him, we will also live with him; if we endure, we will also reign with him; if we deny him, he will also deny us; if we are faithless, he remains faithful—for he cannot deny himself. (2 Tim 2:11–13 NRSV)

The first "if" statement reflects the benefit of responding to the invitation to live in Christ. (This could happen during this life or *after* physical death, according to the hope of Christ-mediated salvation for all, as the person *dies* to sin into new life.) The second "if" statement encourages believers to endure, and the reward is most astounding—reigning with Christ. The third "if" statement changes to the negative consequence of denying Christ. Although this is a very serious warning to Christians, it is not presented as irreversible. The fourth "if" statement contrasts the potential character of humans—*faithless* at times or even for a lifetime—with the steadfast character of Christ. He is *faithful,* even when we are faithless. This changes the pattern from that of the first three statements, in which human actions are followed by consequences, either positive or negative. Another passage affirms God's faithfulness: "What if some were unfaithful? Will their faithlessness nullify the faithfulness of God? By no means!" (Rom 3:3–4 NRSV). God's character is not changed by human folly; faithfulness is an unchanging quality of God. For all who have ever been faithless, this is good news.

The wrath of God is a facet of God's love.

God's wrath is not a vengeful action or vindictive characteristic, seeking to inflict misery for misery's sake. Furthermore, it is certainly not an uncontrollable rage. God's wrath is a purposeful action intended to direct people in a way that fulfills God's purposes.[23] This is a different understanding than what is portrayed by much of traditional theology, which ultimately sees God's wrath as inflicting continuous punishment or torment upon lost sinners forever. Thus, traditional theology is contrary to this scriptural description of God: "He does not retain his anger forever, because he delights in showing clemency" (Mic 7:18 NRSV). By viewing God's wrath as a facet of God's love, we have a much different awareness of who God is. "In God himself love outbalances wrath, for God is angered by human sin, not *although* he loves human beings but *because* he loves them. He says No to sin because he says Yes to the sinner."[24] This is not to say that it is pleasant to experience God's wrath. A proper human response to the prospect of God's wrath is repentance. In Revelation 16, it is implied that the seven bowls of God's wrath are intended to prompt repentance, but the people fail to repent (16:9, 11). These seven plagues "are the last, for with them the wrath of God is ended" (Rev 15:1 NRSV). The potential for repentance by these people on earth has apparently also ended. Nevertheless, as we indicated earlier in this chapter, repentance could be possible, as willed by God, even in the afterlife.

23. See Heschel, *The Prophets,* 358–82.
24. Moltmann, *The Coming of God,* 243.

God's love and God's justice are not competitors.

God's love and justice are sometimes seen in tension. Yet, they must be in harmony, since God is unified in purpose. God's justice is impossible for humans to attain, and no one may enter eternal life with sin. Thus, on that basis all would be excluded from eternal life: "since all have sinned and fall short of the glory of God" (Rom 3:23 NRSV). Even so, God's love has provided the way to eternal life; that is, by his Son and the atonement made by him for us. Redemption demonstrates God's love for humans while employing and achieving justice. "God's judgment separates the sin from the person, condemns the sin and gives the person of the sinner a free pardon. The anger with which the righteous God condemns the unrighteousness which makes people cast themselves and this world into misery is nothing other than an expression of his passionate love."[25] Therefore, when considering the *heart* of God, love and justice are complementary, not in conflict. "Once we see that God's justice is more than mere retribution but is also restorative, and once we see that divine punishments are more than deserved but also corrective, then a way is open to see God's final punishment as another manifestation of this very same justice and not something qualitatively different. It is retributive but also restorative. It is deserved but also corrective."[26] God's love and justice bring about the long-term good of all. Hence, we can trust God and be grateful for the heart of God which is unified in love. "God is love" (1 John 4:16 NRSV). Trusting in the Lord is more than hoping that things will work out. Trusting is knowing—knowing the heart of God. "It was only in the certainty that His mercy is greater than His justice that the prophet could pray: *Though our iniquities testify against us, Act, O Lord, for Thy name's sake* (Jeremiah 14:7)."[27]

God seeks and saves the lost.

Jesus told three parables about seeking and saving the lost, which are recorded in Luke 15. They provide amazing insight into the heart of God, especially considering all three parables together (the *lost sheep* in verves 3–7, the *lost coin* in verses 8–10, and the *lost son* in verses 11–32). The focus of the first parable is on the one lost sheep and the shepherd who leaves

---

25. Ibid.

26. MacDonald, *The Evangelical Universalist*, 138.

27. Heschel, *The Prophet*, 382.

the other ninety-nine sheep to search for it until it is found. Suddenly the story is transformed into a message of repentance and life. "Just so, I tell you, there will be more joy in heaven over one sinner who repents than over ninety-nine righteous persons who need no repentance" (Luke 15:7 NRSV). Just as there is celebration in the story over finding one lost sheep, there is celebration in heaven over one sinner who repents. The question must be raised: if it were not for the improper limits of traditional theology described earlier in this chapter, could the rejoicing in heaven be for those who repent in the afterlife, as well as those who repent in this lifetime? The second parable is about a woman who searches and finds a lost coin (one out of ten). Jesus concludes this parable similarly to the first: "Just so, I tell you, there is joy in the presence of the angels of God over one sinner who repents" (Luke 15:10 NRSV). In both parables, the focus is on finding the one that is lost and restoring everything as a whole.

Rejoicing over the return of the lost.

The third parable is more complex than the two previous ones. Jesus tells a story of a man and his two sons. The younger son asks his father for his share of the inheritance. The father obliges the request, and the son departs for a distant land where he squanders the wealth on loose living. A famine comes upon the land, and the son resorts to tending pigs for a wage that is apparently so low that he longs to eat the pods that the pigs are eating. No one gives him anything to eat. Finally, the son realizes his desperate need, and decides to return to his father, asking to become one of his hired workers. The son prepares the right words to say to his father that will convey his confession and plea for help: "Father, I have sinned against heaven and before you; I am no longer worthy to be called your son; treat me like one of your hired hands" (Luke 15:18–19 NRSV). From a distance the father saw his son coming, felt compassion for him, ran to meet him, and embraced and kissed him. The son said his prepared words but was cut short by his father ordering the servants to bring the best robe for his son, as well as a ring and sandals. The father initiates a celebration and has a fattened calf killed. *The father is overjoyed at his son's return*: "for this son of mine was dead and is alive again; he was lost and is found!' And they began to celebrate" (Luke 15:24 NRSV).

Meanwhile, the older son heard the celebration and learned that his brother had returned. He became angry and refused to enter. Then, his father went out to talk with the older brother, pleading with him. Nevertheless, he responded by citing his loyalty to his father, complaining that he had never even been given so much as a goat so that he could celebrate with his friends. The older brother highlights to his father that "this son of yours" wasted the wealth and even adds that he was with prostitutes. The father, addressing the older brother as "my son," reassures him that everything the father has is his. Then, the father summarizes the reason for the celebration, in essence inviting the older brother to participate in the joy of once again seeing "this brother of yours." For example, "But we had to celebrate and rejoice, because this brother of yours was dead and has come to life; he was lost and has been found" (Luke 15:32 NRSV). For a second time (see 15:24 above), the father says that the younger son "was lost and is found." "However, there is no question that he gets himself lost."[28] This makes the father's compassion, forgiveness, and generosity all the more remarkable—and shows us that the heart of God is focused on all human beings, for all are lost until they come to God through Christ. In a remarkable twist in the parable, the older son is shown to be *lost* when he rejects his father's pleading to rejoice with him in the younger son's return. Thus, the parable interjects a new category of being *lost*. The parable ends without telling us whether the older son responded favorably to his father and reconciled with his brother. Thus, the parable presents a challenge to all who believe they are loyal to God: that is, understand the heart of God, be obedient to Christ, and rejoice that God wants all to be saved.

The heart of God in eternity.

The three parables describe God's love for people and the rejoicing which occurs when one sinner repents (Luke 15:7, 10, 32). Are we to presume, as does traditional theology which holds that eternal punishment for the lost is irreversible and endless, that God's heart for the lost changes after their death? Even more unimaginable, are we to think that God's heart would still pine for the lost people in "eternity," but God would do nothing about it? This view would surely conflict with our understanding of God's sovereignty. Some may say that human choice allows people to reject God and prevents God from fulfilling God's desire that everyone be saved—even though God made humans. Then, we remember that God has known the ramifications of human choice since even before creating the world. The

28. Van Beeck, "'Lost and Found' in Luke 15," 401.

three parables in Luke 15 show that the heart of God is to seek and save the lost. We will explore further in chapters 3 and 4 how biblical truth continues even when theological thinking has faltered.

3

Various Christian Views on Salvation in the Afterlife

THIS CHAPTER EXAMINES A selection of Christian perspectives on the extent of salvation. We begin with twelve church fathers from the ancient and medieval church. Then, we *fast forward* to the twentieth century and encounter works by four prominent theologians on the threshold of Christ-mediated salvation for all.[1]

Church Fathers

This section looks at the views of twelve church fathers who wrote on eternal life and eternal punishment. We will examine specific indications of how they viewed the purpose and duration of eternal punishment, for example, restoration versus torment or endless versus limited in duration. They frequently use *eternal fire*[2] as a reference for eternal punishment. The first four church fathers to be reviewed are Clement of Rome, Ignatius of Antioch, Justin Martyr, and Irenaeus of Lyons from the first and second centuries. The writings of these four church fathers are not specific enough to assess their views on the purpose and duration of eternal punishment.[3]

1. For more extensive reviews of Christian perspectives on this topic, see MacDonald, "All Shall Be Well"; Ramelli, *The Christian Doctrine of the Apokatastasis*.

2. Biblical references to *eternal fire* or *fire of hell* include Matthew 18:8, 9; 25:41; Mark 9:43, 48.

3. While other church fathers would also fall into this category, these four are described to demonstrate some of the earliest views and the overall diversity among the

Then beginning with Clement of Alexandria and Tertullian from the second and third centuries, the church fathers' views are quite specific. All in all, there is great diversity in how the church fathers view God's purposes for *eternal fire* and eternal punishment.

Clement of Rome lived in the late first century.

He composed "Letter to the Corinthians," the only work authenticated as his writing. Clement wrote: "Since then all things are seen and heard [by God], let us fear Him, and forsake those wicked works which proceed from evil desires; so that, through His mercy, we may be protected from the judgments to come."[4] Although he warns of upcoming judgments, Clement does not indicate whether these judgments will come during this lifetime or the next, and he does not articulate a view on the nature and purpose of eternal punishment.

Ignatius of Antioch (ca 50–ca 98–117).

Ignatius warned against false teachers in his "Epistle to the Ephesians" 16 and wrote: "Such a one becoming defiled [in this way], shall go away into everlasting fire, and so shall every one that hearkens unto him."[5] Since the specific context is false teaching, Ignatius' general view of the purpose of eternal punishment is unknown. The reference to everlasting fire is not clear whether it means to be sent into the fire and stay there forever, or to be sent for some undesignated duration into the fire that burns forever.

Justin Martyr (ca 100–ca 165).

Justin wrote about the eternal fire in *The First Apology*: "Every man will suffer punishment in eternal fire according to the merit of his deed, and will render account according to the power he has received from God, as Christ intimated when He said, 'To whom God has given more, of him shall more be required [Luke 12:48].'"[6] Justin seems to be stressing the degree of punishment according to deeds. It is unclear whether he believes such

church fathers.

4. Clement of Rome, "Letter to the Corinthians," 28.
5. Ignatius of Antioch, "Epistle to the Ephesians," 16.
6. Justin Martyr, *The First Apology*, 17.

punishment is everlasting or ends after the person has endured sufficient suffering for wrongs, the length of which could vary by individual.

Irenaeus of Lyons (ca 130–ca 200).

Irenaeus wrote *Against Heresies*, in which he said: "And this is what has been spoken by the prophet, I am a jealous God, making peace, and creating evil things [Isaiah 45:7]; thus making peace and friendship with those who repent and turn to Him, and bringing [them to] unity, but preparing for the impenitent, those who shun the light, eternal fire and outer darkness, which are evils indeed to those persons who fall into them."[7] Irenaeus is making the point that it is the same God making peace with those who repent and preparing the eternal fire for those who shun the light. Among the first four church fathers, this is the most direct statement of the purpose of eternal punishment. However, Irenaeus does not address the duration of eternal punishment. While he makes explicit mention of eternal fire and outer darkness, he does not indicate whether people would remain in these *evils* forever or temporarily.

Clement of Alexandria (ca 150–ca 215).

Clement, a predecessor of Origen at the theological school of Alexandria, expressed a concept of universal restoration which was later developed by Origen and Gregory of Nyssa.[8] Clement bases his concept on the belief that the Son is Savior and Lord of both those who have believed and those who have not believed. "And how is He Saviour and Lord, if not the Saviour and Lord of all? But He is the Saviour of those who have believed, because of their wishing to know; and the Lord of those who have not believed, till, being enabled to confess him, they obtain the peculiar and appropriate boon which comes by Him."[9]

Clement believed that human freedom would remain as the Lord restored all persons to salvation. Virtue is the key motivation within human freedom. "Everything, then, which did not hinder a man's choice from being free, He made and rendered auxiliary to virtue, in order that there might be revealed somehow or other, even to those capable of seeing but dimly, the

---

7. Irenaeus of Lyons, *Against Heresies*, 4:40:1.

8. Harmon, *Every Knee Should Bow*, 19, 37.

9. Clement of Alexandria, *The Stromata*, 7:2.

one only almighty, good God—from eternity to eternity saving by His Son. And, on the other hand, He is in no respect whatever the cause of evil. For all things are arranged with a view to the salvation of the universe by the Lord of the universe, both generally and particularly."[10] Nonetheless, Clement thought that humans would need corrections by God and they would need to repent in order to be restored and receive salvation. "But necessary corrections, through the goodness of the great overseeing Judge, both by the attendant angels, and by various acts of anticipative judgment, and by the perfect judgment, compel egregious sinners to repent."[11]

In another writing, Clement seems to espouse a view of everlasting punishment for the wicked: "All souls are immortal, even those of the wicked, for whom it were better that they were not deathless. For, punished with the endless vengeance of quenchless fire, and not dying, it is impossible for them to have a period put to their misery."[12] Since this text is a fragment unto itself, it is not possible to determine its context. Still, there is a plausible way to reconcile the two writings. Since *The Stomata* reveals Clement's belief that sinners will be corrected by God and then they will repent, the text from *Fragments* could support this view in that God, not the sinner, would put an end to the misery of the eternal fire—after, that is, correction and repentance have come about. Thus, the weight of the evidence suggests that Clement of Alexandria believed that the judgment of God was for correction and that ultimately humans would repent of their sins and be restored eternally by God's goodness and authority as Lord of all.

Tertullian (ca 160–ca 225).

For Tertullian, those faithful to God will be "clothed upon with the proper substance of eternity; but the profane, and all who are not true worshippers of God, in like manner shall be consigned to the punishment of everlasting fire—that fire which, from its very nature indeed, directly ministers to their incorruptibility."[13] Thus, he views the eternal punishment to be everlasting and the essence of the wicked to remain unchanged throughout eternity. To emphasize his point, Tertullian describes the state as "the endless judgment

---

10. Ibid.

11. Ibid.

12. Clement of Alexandria, "From the Book of Soul."

13. Tertullian, *The Apology*, 48.

which still supplies punishment with fuel!"[14] It is clear that Tertullian views eternal punishment as endless and even refers to it as torment as he and others faithful to God understand "the greatness of the threatened torment, not merely long-enduring but everlasting."[15]

Origen (ca 185–ca 254).

Origen is known for his theology of *apokatastasis*, that is, universal restoration, in which all created beings will be restored to their intended harmony with God. Origen developed perhaps the first systematic theology, which is called *De Principiis (On First Principles)*.[16] A summary of *On First Principles* is provided later in this chapter. Here we want to observe Origen's view specifically on "the meaning of the threatening of eternal fire."[17] The fire results from a person's sins, chastising the person.

> When the soul has gathered together a multitude of evil works, and an abundance of sins against itself, at a suitable time all that assembly of evils boils up to punishment, and is set on fire to chastisements; when the mind itself, or conscience, receiving by divine power into the memory all those things of which it had stamped on itself certain signs and forms at the moment of sinning, will see a kind of history, as it were, of all the foul, and shameful, and unholy deeds which it has done, exposed before its eyes: then is the conscience itself harassed, and, pierced by its own goads, becomes an accuser and a witness against itself. And this, I think, was the opinion of the Apostle Paul himself, when he said, Their thoughts mutually accusing or excusing them in the day when God will judge the secrets of men by Jesus Christ, according to my Gospel. From which it is understood that around the substance of the soul certain tortures are produced by the hurtful affections of sins themselves.[18]

Thus, Origen is describing eternal punishment as a process of chastisement, in which the conscience becomes aware of sins. As we will see in the next section "More on Origen and *Apokatastasis*," Origen develops a view ultimately leading to universal restoration.

14. Ibid.

15. Ibid., 45.

16. Greggs, "Apokatastasis," 30.

17. Origen, *De Principiis*, 2:10:3.

18. Ibid., 2:10:4.

Basil the Great (ca 330–379).

Basil describes the ultimate condition of those who have received the Holy Spirit and have been faithful to God. "They, then, that were sealed by the Spirit unto the day of redemption, and preserve pure and undiminished the first fruits which they received of the Spirit, are they that shall hear the words 'well done thou good and faithful servant; you have been faithful over a few things, I will make you ruler over many things' [Matthew 25:21]."[19] Then, Basil contrasts the condition of those who have grieved the Holy Spirit by their unfaithfulness. "In like manner they which have grieved the Holy Spirit by the wickedness of their ways, or have not wrought for Him that gave to them, shall be deprived of what they have received, their grace being transferred to others; or, according to one of the evangelists, they shall even be wholly cut asunder, [Matthew 24:51]—the cutting asunder meaning complete separation from the Spirit."[20] To this Basil adds that the separation of the Holy Spirit from the unfaithful shall continue in hell. "He [the Spirit] will be wholly cut off from the soul that has defiled His grace. For this reason 'In Hell there is none that makes confession; in death none that remembers God,' because the succor of the Spirit is no longer present."[21] Basil's statements about separation and inability to confess specifically refer to those who received the Spirit, then grieved the Spirit. In Basil's view, when these people are in hell, they will not even remember God. While Basil may have concluded that the same fate awaited people who had never come to Christ, his views about such people are not stated. Moreover, Basil's view is centered on people's abject incapacity in hell (*they cannot confess; they cannot remember God*). Basil's view on eternal punishment can be summarized in two parts: for those who had received the Spirit but then grieved the Spirit, after death they are separated from the Spirit; for those who had never received the Spirit, Basil's view on eternal punishment is unspecified. For the purpose of this review, considering his strong beliefs about the Holy Spirit not being present for those who had grieved the Spirit, it is concluded that Basil may be included in the category of church fathers who held to a view of everlasting punishment.

---

19. Basil the Great, *De Spiritu Santo*, 40.
20. Ibid.
21. Ibid.

Gregory of Nazianzus (329–389).

Gregory refers to Jesus as the *Fire* who cleanses the righteous. "For I know a cleansing fire which Christ came to send upon the earth [Luke 12:49], and He Himself is anagogically called a Fire. This Fire takes away whatsoever is material and of evil habit. . . ."[22] Gregory also refers to other types of fire which God uses against sinners such as at Sodom, Satan, Satan's angels, and the Lord's enemies. In addition, there is "one even more fearful still than these, the unquenchable fire which is ranged with the worm that dies not but is eternal for the wicked. For all these belong to the destroying power; though some may prefer even in this place to take a more merciful view of this fire, worthily of Him that chastises."[23] Therefore, even though Gregory specifies that the eternal fire applies to the wicked, he acknowledges that chastisement is more in accord with the qualities of God. Thus, Gregory perceives that God may use fire for cleansing or for destruction. It is not clear whether Gregory believes that eternal punishment is everlasting. He seems to prefer to acknowledge that there is more than one way to view the eternal fire. In Gregory we see a church father who understands and engages in the debate over the various purposes of fire in Scripture. He acknowledges the view of everlasting punishment, but he seems to prefer to focus on the purposes of God, including chastisement together with mercy.

Gregory of Nyssa (ca 330–ca 395).

Gregory believed that God's purpose for the eternal fire is not for punishment, but for purging the individual of sin and evil. "Then it seems, I said, that it is not punishment chiefly and principally that the Deity, as Judge, afflicts sinners with; but He operates, as your argument has shown, only to get the good separated from the evil and to attract it into the communion of blessedness."[24] Nonetheless, the fire would feel like punishment to the person undergoing the purging process. In fact, the agony experienced by persons with greater amounts of evil in them would be more than that experienced by persons with relatively small amounts of evil. "That, said the Teacher, is my meaning; and also that the agony will be measured by the amount of evil there is in each individual."[25] At the end of the process,

22. Gregory of Nazianzus, "Oration 40," 36.

23. Ibid.

24. Gregory of Nyssa, *On the Soul and the Resurrection*, 66.

25. Ibid., 67.

evil will be eliminated from each person so that only good comes forth and restoration will follow. "His [God's] end is one, and one only; it is this: when the complete whole of our race shall have been perfected from the first man to the last—some having at once in this life been cleansed from evil, others having afterwards in the necessary periods been healed by the Fire, others having in their life here been unconscious equally of good and of evil—to offer to every one of us participation in the blessings which are in Him, which, the Scripture tells us, eye has not seen, nor ear heard, nor thought ever reached."[26] Thus, Gregory holds a view of universal restoration similar to that of Origen. Furthermore, Gregory details a process of purgation which will take place before each person who dies with evil in them proceeds to the restored state of blessedness.

John Chrysostom (ca 347–407).

John views the eternal fire as never ceasing, unlike fire in this world. "For when you hear of fire, do not suppose the fire in that world to be like this: for fire in this world burns up and makes away with anything which it takes hold of; but that fire is continually burning those who have once been seized by it, and never ceases: therefore also is it called unquenchable."[27] Moreover, John portrays the punishment as too horrible to describe. "For those also who have sinned must put on immortality, not for honour, but to have a constant supply of material for that punishment to work upon; and how terrible this is, speech could never depict. . . ."[28] The loss of good things that people have known on earth would be punishment enough in hell "that even if no other kind of punishment were appointed for those who sin here, it would of itself be sufficient to vex us more bitterly than the torments in hell, and to confound our souls."[29] Clearly, John views eternal punishment as everlasting and sees hell as torment.

26. Ibid., 87.

27. John Chrysostom, *Two Exhortations to Theodore After His Fall*, "Letter 1," 10.

28. Ibid.

29. Ibid.

Augustine of Hippo (354–430).

Augustine taught that the eternal punishment of the lost was everlasting torment.

> It is in vain, then, that some, indeed very many, make moan over the eternal punishment, and perpetual, unintermitted torments of the lost, and say they do not believe it shall be so; not, indeed, that they directly oppose themselves to Holy Scripture, but, at the suggestion of their own feelings, they soften down everything that seems hard, and give a milder turn to statements which they think are rather designed to terrify than to be received as literally true.[30]

Augustine's statement indicates that many during his time and perhaps before his time did not believe that punishment after death was endless, as he deems to be the literal meaning of Scripture. His observation confirms a major point to be made summarizing this section. There were indeed divergent views related to the meaning of eternal punishment at least until the time of Augustine. Curiously, however, he believes that some punishments are temporary, even after death, while other punishments are everlasting.

> But temporary punishments are suffered by some in this life only, by others after death, by others both now and then; but all of them before that last and strictest judgment. But of those who suffer temporary punishments after death, all are not doomed to those everlasting pains which are to follow that judgment ; for to some, as we have already said, what is not remitted in this world is remitted in the next, that is, they are not punished with the eternal punishment of the world to come.[31]

Augustine seems to be saying that some punishment after death will be inflicted even on those who are saved; this temporary punishment, which is purgatorial, would take place before the judgment. More will be said about Augustine and his influence on theology later in this chapter.

Summary of Church Fathers on eternal punishment.

In this section, we observed the diversity of views of twelve church fathers on the purpose of eternal fire or eternal punishment: whether they

---

30. Augustine, *The Handbook on Faith, Hope and Love*, 112
31. Augustine, *City of God*, 21:13.

considered it as corrective and restorative, as everlasting punishment (even torment), or another view. Their views may be summarized as follows:

1. Corrective and restorative: Clement of Alexandria, Origen, Gregory of Nazianzus,[32] Gregory of Nyssa, "very many" in Augustine's day[33]

2. Everlasting punishment or torment: Tertullian, Basil of Caesarea,[34] John Chrysostom, Augustine

3. Unclear: Clement of Rome, Ignatius of Antioch, Justin Martyr, Irenaeus

As shown in this summary and throughout this section, the church fathers held a wide variety of views through the fifth century. This diversity would change dramatically around the sixth century for reasons explained in the next two sections: condemnation of certain views espoused by Origen and increased acceptance of Augustine's view of everlasting torment for the lost.

More on Origen and Apokatastasis

Summary of Origen's theology as presented in De Principiis.[35]

In *De Principiis* Preface, Origen asserts that the truth comes through the Word of God, meaning both Jesus Christ and the Scriptures. He alludes to some people who do not rightly make use of the truth, and contends that more understanding is needed in many areas of theology. Thus, the context is his desire to present his ideas, hypotheses, and questions to advance the development of doctrine. Origen is confident that by relying on the Word

---

32. Gregory of Nazianzus indicated that there is more than one way to view the eternal fire, but he seems to prefer the view which acknowledges God's purposes of chastisement and mercy.

33. See the section above on Augustine of Hippo and his statement in *The Handbook on Faith, Hope and Love* 112, "that some, indeed *very many*, make moan over the eternal punishment, and perpetual, unintermitted torments of the lost" (*emphasis added*).

34. Although Basil did not specifically address the eternal fate of those who had not received the Holy Spirit, it is concluded that Basil's views are most closely associated with the church fathers who held to a view of everlasting punishment.

35. This section summarizes Origen's *De Principiis* Preface–2, particularly as they relate to *apokatastasis*.

of God, the truth will become known. Implied in his commentary is that by sharing ideas, those who are genuinely searching for truth will find it.

The range of theological topics covered by Origen's work is vast, and he conveys his ideas by referencing Scripture and using logic. To Origen, the mind is of critical importance. Christ is wisdom and truth. He reflects God to us and provides the way to the Father. Origen observes that human beings are not static; they may move closer to the truth or fall from it. On the other hand, some angels and other powers seem to continue in a holy state, while others such as Lucifer have fallen away. Origen contends that human beings can reach a continuous perfect state, by the power of God. Along the way, one may slip and then resume moving upward. Nevertheless, it is by human free choice that some turn away from God.

Origen qualifies his intention: the chapter on "The End or Consummation" is his speculation for discussion purposes. "Now we ourselves speak on these subjects with great fear and caution, discussing and investigating rather than laying down fixed and certain conclusions."[36] Origen believes that at the end of the world every person will be judged for their sins. Some persons have fallen more than others. Nevertheless, every person will be subject to Christ, who gives salvation. For Origen, salvation ultimately comes from the goodness of God, by which everyone is restored through subjection to Christ. Depending on the translation, Origen envisions that even the devil and his angels could be restored. Universal restoration, according to Origen, fulfills the scriptural passage which concludes that "God may be all in all" (1 Cor 15:28 NRSV).

Origen extends his discussion to other created beings. Regarding the sun, moon and stars, he asks whether it is proper to consider them as "rational beings" and whether their souls will be freed at the end of the age. He reasons that whatever is true for humans may be applied to these "heavenly beings." After all "we know that the whole creation has been groaning. . . ." (Rom 8:22 NRSV). Regarding angels, Origen asserts that they can only be made holy by the Holy Spirit, while their assignments are made according to merit. Even so, some angels have fallen, as did the devil.

Origen notes that humans have been given free choice. While this condition allows people to stray from God, it also is a strong motivation for their return. God has designed creation so that everything will be restored. This process may be lengthy, involving one world after another. Each successive world is an age. At each age, there is pain for those who do not obey

36. Origen, *De Principiis*, 1:6:1.

God and healing for those who accept God's teaching. This world may be the culmination of the ages because Christ "has appeared once for all at the end of the ages to do away with sin by the sacrifice of himself" (Heb 9:26 NIV). Then again, Origen observes that Ephesians 2:7 mentions ages to come. In either case, ultimately all things will be restored.

Origen affirms that the God of the new covenant is the same God of the old covenant. God is both just and good. When afflictions occur, they may represent God's remedy to bring people back from sin. Those who have sinned more need more severe measures to be restored.

Origen asserts that every living creature, the number of which is finite and known by God, has a soul. It is the soul which can return to its beginning condition. God created every human being (and all living beings) in the circumstances in which they were born. Life is no accident. Human free will corresponds with the principle of merit. To illustrate, Origen says that God's love for Jacob over Esau may be explained by Jacob's merit from a former life. Thus, a person's purpose and circumstances in this life may be determined by how that person lived in a previous life.

To Origen, the eternal fire of judgment is not just punishment, but has a cleansing effect. A person's conscience will then be able to see his or her wrongs for what they are. Then, God will restore the person with healing. For those who have not received proper instruction in this life, but who have performed good deeds, a kind of remedial instruction will be provided. In this way, humans can progress to perfection, sustained by "the contemplation and understanding of God."[37]

Origen's view involves human progress from one world, or age, to the next, finally reaching perfection in the truth of Christ and the goodness of God. While Origen's model relies on a significant element of human merit in order for human progress to occur, it remains grounded in Christ and God. In a similar manner, even though Origen holds that human will continues to operate, he strongly asserts the sovereignty and power of God. Origen's foundation in Christ and God is the key element of his quest to explore extraordinary depths of truth.

37. Ibid., 2:11:7.

Rulings on Origen's views at the
Second Council of Constantinople.

From what we have seen in the previous section, Origen's theology included the pre-existence and transmigration of souls from one world or age to the next. This part of his theology, in particular, was condemned by the Second Council of Constantinople, also known as the Fifth Ecumenical Council, which met in 553. However, the question of whether Origen and the idea of *apokatastasis* where condemned is less settled. "Were Origen and Origenism anathematized? Many learned writers believe so; an equal number deny that they were condemned; most modern authorities are either undecided or reply with reservations."[38] Whether Origen and the idea of *apokatastasis* were condemned by the Second Constantinople Council, or whether only certain aspects of Origen's theology were condemned, either way the result was certainly to dampen interest and enthusiasm for *apokatastasis* and perhaps to convince many that the idea was heretical.

It is instructive to review a perspective which holds that only certain aspects of Origen's theology were condemned, but the idea of *apokatastasis* itself was not condemned. This perspective observes that the condemnations of *apokatastasis* were linked with other questionable theological ideas. "Even in the anathemas against Origen associated (in some manner) with the Fifth Ecumenical Council, the objection seems not to have been with a universal restoration per se but rather with the protology presupposed by the Origenist version of universal restoration, as Anathema I suggests: 'If anyone asserts the fabulous pre-existence of souls, and shall assert the monstrous restoration (*apokatastasis*) which follows from it, let him be an anathema.'"[39] This pattern of linking specific issues of concern to universal restoration is observed in the other anathemas. "It is clear that when *apokatastasis* is condemned in the fifteen canons it is always done in association with other, problematic, ideas."[40]

The council's anathemas condemning certain aspects of Origen's theology of universal restoration, in part, related to its later development by others.[41] Since Origen died in 254, the rulings of the Second Constantinople

38. *Catholic Encyclopedia*, "Second Origenistic Crisis."

39. Harmon, *Every Knee*, 132.

40. MacDonald, "Introduction: Between Heresy and Dogma," *"All Shall Be Well"* 8.

41. MacDonald cites Didymus the Blind, Evagrius of Pontus, Philoxenus, and Stephen Bar Sudaili, see ibid., 7.

Council came nearly three hundred years after his death. It would also seem to be noteworthy that "ten years before the fifth ecumenical council, the emperor Justinian I (emperor from 527–565) convened a local Synod in Constantinople condemning Origen's heresies in nine anathemas. . . . Although the later council's anathemas did vindicate *most* of what Justinian wrote they do qualify his apparent *blanket* condemnation of *apokatastasis*. . . ."[42] Thus, apparently the council did not condemn universal restoration as a theological idea, rather only certain aspects of it. As an observation, there was an apparent mixing of political and religious authorities in the decisions. The political motivation could have been to control the empire by a narrower theological scope of salvation than presented by universal restoration. Presumably the religious authorities were guided by a scriptural approach which allowed universal restoration to remain as a theological concept, after they stripped away extraneous issues.

Finally, additional evidence supporting the viewpoint that universal restoration itself was not condemned comes from observing the church's favorable treatment of Gregory of Nyssa, who further developed universal restoration after Origen. Gregory lived in the fourth century, well before the Second Constantinople Council. "It is significant that Gregory of Nyssa, who developed a concept of *apokatastasis* virtually identical to that of Origen sans Origen's protology, was never condemned by council or synod, was revered by the later church as a staunch defender of Nicene orthodoxy, and was canonized as a saint with a feast day on March 9. . . ."[43] Therefore, one might think that Christ-mediated salvation for all would have engaged a lively discussion among Christian theologians in the centuries following the Second Constantinople Council. Instead, it seems to have been relegated to a minority of Christian thinkers and believers.

One reason for the diminished level of interest may be found in the nature of the council itself. The major item on its agenda concerned a Christological issue (two natures in the one person of Christ) that was still being debated one hundred years after it was decided at the Council at Chalcedon, held in 451.[44] Therefore, the anathemas against Origen's universal restoration, with modifications by his followers, may not have received as much widespread attention as the Christological issue at the Second Constantinople Council. Perhaps more importantly, "one result

42. Ibid.

43. Harmon, *Every Knee*, 132.

44. Gonzalez, *The Story of Christianity*, vol. 1, 256–8, 413.

of the ambiguity about whether the council had condemned all forms of universalism or simply Origenist *apokatastasis* was that from this point on Christians avoided anything that looked remotely Origenist. In the Western church this impulse was reinforced by the enormous influence of Augustine's theology, which was emphatic about the eternal conscious torment of the lost."[45] It is to Augustine and his theology regarding eternal punishment that we turn next.

More on Augustine and His View of Everlasting Torment

Augustine's rising influence can be illustrated during the papacy of Gregory the Great, who became pope in 590 at the end of the same century when certain aspects of Origen's theology were condemned. In contrast to the treatment of Origen's ideas by the Second Constantinople Council, "what for Augustine was conjecture, in Gregory became certainty. Thus, for instance, the theologian of Hippo had suggested the possibility that there was a place of purification for those who died in sin, where they would spend some time before going to heaven. On the basis of these speculations of Augustine, Gregory affirmed the existence of such a place, and thus gave impetus to the development of the doctrine of purgatory."[46] The idea of purgatory sounds much like what is found in the writings of Clement of Alexandria, Origen, and Gregory of Nyssa with respect to purging, correction, and restoration. Nonetheless, purgatory is a place essentially for those who died as participants in the church receiving the means of grace through it, whereas the purging and restoration envisioned by the three above-mentioned church fathers was for all humanity. Thus, the eternal fate of those who die outside the faith was unaltered by the doctrine of purgatory; Augustine's idea of everlasting conscious torment for the lost continued on, as it largely does today.

Augustine's view of everlasting torment is related to his belief in predestination:

> For if all had remained under the punishment of just condemnation, there would have been seen in no one the mercy of redeeming grace. And, on the other hand, if all had been transferred from darkness to light, the severity of retribution would have been manifested in

45. MacDonald, "Introduction: Between Heresy and Dogma," 9.

46. Gonzalez, *The Story of Christianity*, vol. 1, 247.

none. But many more are left under punishment than are delivered from it, in order that it may thus be shown what was due to all."[47]

The logical consequence of predestination, in addition to some being saved and the others condemned, would be that those who are condemned eternally would face an endless punishment. Otherwise, if they could be saved after death, there would be no lasting predestination in two distinct eternal states, as Augustine has described.

Protestant reformer John Calvin picked up Augustine's idea of predestination and developed a systematic theology from it. Indeed Augustine's ideas have been used pervasively in the Western church. "Throughout the Middle Ages, no theologian was quoted more often than he was, and he became one of the great doctors of the Roman Catholic Church. But he was also the favorite theologian of the great Protestant reformers of the sixteenth century. Thus, Augustine, variously interpreted, has become the most influential theologian in the entire Western church, both Protestant and Catholic."[48] After fifteen centuries, it is time to reevaluate Augustine's view that eternal punishment for the lost means everlasting torment. Just as the church fathers expressed a diversity of views on the possibility of salvation after death, we should be willing to explore biblical truths and theological perspectives which point to *the way, the truth, and the life.*

More on the Historical Theology of Purgatory

The Roman Catholic doctrine of purgatory reflects a need for purification after death. By contrast, Eastern Orthodoxy, which was involved in the first major church split with the Roman Catholic Church in 1054, does not agree with the doctrine of purgatory.[49] Nonetheless, some Orthodox theologians do accept a concept of purgatory.[50] During the Reformation, Protestants rejected the idea of purgatory because they found no biblical basis for it. In addition, Reformers objected to purgatory because it relied on a concept of merit which in part could be earned by people to shorten the time in purgatory and it was linked to an extensive money-producing venture for the Roman Church.

---

47. Augustine, *City of God*, 21:12.

48. Gonzalez, *The Story of Christianity*, vol. 1, 216.

49. Walls, *The Oxford Handbook of Eschatology*, 242–3.

50. Placher, *Essentials of Christian Theology*, 382.

Many Protestants and Evangelicals today associate purgatory with the sale of indulgences because this practice was assailed by Martin Luther in his Ninety-five Theses, which he nailed to the Castle Church door in Wittenberg in 1517. "The theology which underpinned indulgences rested on the doctrine of the treasury of merits. Christ, by his sacrifice on the cross, created an inexhaustible store of merit, to which is added that of the martyrs and saints."[51] One might wonder: if Christ created an inexhaustible amount of merit, why was there a need for additional merit from individual Christians, whether martyrs, saints, or other believers? In any case, according to Roman Catholic belief, the Church could distribute merit in the form of indulgences, which provided forgiveness of sins and therefore a shortened stay in purgatory. Even though indulgences were the specific objection of Luther's Ninety-five Theses, Roman Church practices had already linked merit and money to reduced time in purgatory.

A substantial amount of money and property contributions were made to the Roman Church over several centuries in exchange for masses being held and prayers being said to reduce the time that a donor or loved one would spend in purgatory. This practice was part of a larger system of merit which flowed from the Roman Church. "Human beings could construct their own humble imitations of the mercy of God in good works. Some of these were works of mercy, such as giving to beggars or contributing to the upkeep of the hospitals which looked after the chronically sick or elderly."[52] The Church determined the types of good works which contributed to the merit of the individual and which in turn could count toward reducing the amount of time spent in purgatory.

The acquisition of personal merit is not in step with the biblical concept of justification by God's grace through faith. Righteousness comes to each believer from Jesus Christ. For a view of purgatory which does coincide with the exclusive work of God in the process of human perfection, we turn to the vision of Catherine of Genoa (1447–1510). Catherine, who was named a saint by the Roman Church 227 years after her death, provides a unique perspective of purgatory. "She was beatified in 1675 by Clement X, but not canonized till 1737, by Clement XII. Meantime, her writings had been examined by the Holy Office and pronounced to contain doctrine that would be enough, in itself, to prove her sanctity."[53] Yet, as we will

---

51. Tingle, *Purgatory and Piety in Brittany 1480–1720*, 209.

52. MacCulloch, *The Reformation*, 13.

53. *Catholic Encyclopedia*, "St. Catherine of Genoa."

see by examining her vision of purgatory, her understanding of purgatory differed from that of the Roman Church in that her vision did not allow for human efforts to reduce time in purgatory. God alone brings about human perfection and movement through purgatory.

Catherine of Genoa's vision of purgatory.

Catherine of Genoa was born into aristocracy, and her husband was also an aristocrat. They dedicated themselves to helping the poor at a hospital in Genoa, and she served as its director for six years.[54] Nonetheless, it is as a mystic that she is remembered today. Catherine's friends completed her works, including her vision of purgatory, by 1522 although some of her experiences and teachings may have been written while she was still living.[55] Apparently, Catherine's friends were impressed with what she told them about her mystical experience and wanted to preserve it for others. There is no indication that she or they promoted it as a theological work; however, to some extent it has become such. It was probably not written in response to the Reformation although it did have some influence during that period.

Catherine of Genoa experienced the purification and love of God before God showed her the conditions in which souls go through purgatory. Catherine's mystical encounter is described that she "experienced the fiery love of God, a love that consumed her, cleansing and purifying all, so that once quitted this life she could appear forthwith in God's presence."[56] This position then allowed her to see the process by which souls came to God for cleansing before moving on to paradise. Therefore, she presents a unique perspective of the afterlife.

The reason that souls go through purgatory is to be cleansed of sin so that they are purified before entering into the presence of God in heaven. Souls suffer in purgatory, yet they do not feel guilt and they do not know that the suffering is due to their sin, which is compared to rust—an impediment which must be removed gradually. Souls do not sin in purgatory, so no further cleansing is needed other than for original sin and actual sins committed on earth. Each soul has an instinct for God, and souls in purgatory respond to the love of God. There is a fire within each soul in

---

54. Catherine of Genoa, *Purgation and Purgatory, The Spiritual Dialogue*, XV.

55. Ibid., XV.

56. Ibid., 71.

purgatory—like the fire in hell. The fire purifies the soul so that it can perceive God. The suffering in purgatory is overshadowed by God's love.

God has placed no doors on paradise, and God is waiting to receive each person. Anyone can enter, but because of impediments they do not want to do so. God is in control of the entire process, and entering the final phase, the soul is with God at God's initiative. God's love brings about perfection in each soul—perfection that is beyond anything that humans can know on earth. Perfecting souls is necessary even though Jesus Christ's sacrifice on the cross satisfied the justice of God. In the process of purification, souls suffer because they are willing to suffer as they look to God's mercy and they experience joy at the same time as they suffer. The comforts relied on by the soul are gradually removed until the only comfort felt is God. The soul would not want to leave this position. When God sees the soul as pure as it was in its original state, God draws it in with a fiery love and continues to transform the soul until it is perfect—like gold refined completely. With this intense personal attention, God completes the final perfection of the soul—perfection beyond human understanding—and the soul enjoys God and is at rest in God. Thus, the soul moved through purgatory to paradise—and it is God who did it.

Significance of Catherine's vision.

Catherine's version of purgatory differs notably from that of the Roman Church teachings. To her, neither alms nor indulgences could reduce the time spent in purgatory. "And if the living were to offer alms for the benefit of the souls in purgatory, to shorten the assigned time of their purgation, still those souls could not turn with affection to watch, but would leave all things to God, who is paid as He wishes."[57] Therefore, it is implicit that if the souls in purgatory trust in God, so should the living trust God, not human works. Catherine's vision understands indulgences in a similar manner. "Do not rely on yourself and say, 'I will confess myself, receive a plenary indulgence, and with that be cleansed of all my sins.'"[58] Further, the vision warns against insincere or incomplete confession and contrition, which results in a false sense of grace. In general, these admonitions are relevant to Christians and others even today: trust not in yourself or what you do, but only in God.

57. Ibid., 82.
58. Ibid., 84.

Catherine described the soul's passage through purgatory as controlled by God, not by the church. Although sixteenth-century Reformers rejected purgatory, Catherine's vision is worth considering today even by Evangelicals and other Protestants because it does not include extraneous elements added by the Roman Church. Instead of thinking of Catherine's vision as relating strictly to purgatory, it may be helpful to consider it in a more general sense of purification. Then, its relevance may be seen to aid the development of theology today.

The Descent of Christ into Hell

The descent of Jesus Christ into hell relates to the questions about eternal punishment. The Apostles' Creed includes these phrases about Jesus: "[He] was crucified, dead and buried: He descended into hell: The third day He rose again from the dead."[59] Thus, according to the creed, Jesus descended into hell after his death and before he rose from the dead. The Church refers to this period of time as Holy Saturday. The day has bearing on this analysis since the vision that prompted my study came to me on Holy Saturday, April 3, 1999.

Ephesians 4:7–10.

The scriptural basis for Jesus' descent into hell includes Ephesians 4:7–10.

> But each of us was given grace according to the measure of Christ's gift. Therefore it is said, "When he ascended on high he made captivity itself a captive; he gave gifts to his people." (When it says, "He ascended," what does it mean but that he had also descended into the lower parts of the earth? He who descended is the same one who ascended far above all the heavens, so that he might fill all things). (Eph 4:7–10 NRSV)

The quotation in 4:8 "When he ascended on high . . ." refers to Psalm 68:18 speaking about the Lord God, "You ascended the high mount, leading captives in your train and receiving gifts from people, even from those who rebel against the Lord God's abiding there" (Ps 68:18 NRSV). Notice that in Psalm 68, the gifts are received *from* people, whereas in Ephesians, Christ gives gifts *to* his people. Following Ephesians 4:10, Christ bestows grace on

---

59 The Apostles' Creed, www.ccel.org/creeds/apostles.creed.html.

certain Christian leaders to build up the body of Christ. Thus, the Ephesians passage emphasizes that Christ gives grace. Since the passage refers to Christ's descent to hell, it leaves open the question of whether on Holy Saturday Christ gave grace to people in hell. The next passage to be reviewed, 1 Peter 3:18–20, addresses this question.

As one further important note before proceeding, Ephesians 4:9 states that Christ "descended into the lower parts of the earth"—which is a reference to Hades or hell. When combined with Christ's ascent into the heavens in 4:10, Jesus Christ has filled all parts of the universe, from the heavens to hell. This emphasizes Christ's authority everywhere including in hell. Since Christ has such vast authority and since Christ can give grace, it is quite conceivable that Christ can give grace to those in hell. This point is of vital significance as we move forward in this study of what is God's intention for those who are lost.

First Peter 3:18–4:6.

In the first part of this passage, 1 Peter 3:18–20, we see a second reference to Christ's descent into hell on Holy Saturday. To see the context, here is 1 Peter 3:18–22:

> For Christ also suffered for sins once for all, the righteous for the unrighteous, in order to bring you to God. He was put to death in the flesh, but made alive in the spirit, in which also he went and made a proclamation to the spirits in prison, who in former times did not obey, when God waited patiently in the days of Noah, during the building of the ark, in which a few, that is, eight persons, were saved through water. And baptism, which this prefigured, now saves you—not as a removal of dirt from the body, but as an appeal to God for a good conscience, through the resurrection of Jesus Christ, who has gone into heaven and is at the right hand of God, with angels, authorities, and powers made subject to him. (1 Pet 3:18–22 NRSV)

There is much disagreement among biblical scholars and theologians as to the meaning of verses 19 and 20. One disagreement is whether "spirits in prison" refers to people (and their status) or disobedient angelic spirits. In order to understand this passage, it is important to keep in mind why 1 Peter was written, that is, to encourage the readers to live for God, even in suffering. First Peter 3:18 invokes Christ as the ultimate inspiration. "For Christ also suffered [died]. . .." Christ does not need to die again—he died once; his work is finished. He suffered and died as one who is "righteous for the unrighteous." The readers, who were once among the unrighteous, can also accomplish good if they are righteous in Christ. Moreover, Christ suffered and died for a precious purpose, that is, "to bring you to God." Knowing that God values them is a strong motivation for the readers to demonstrate faith and courage. Finally, still in 3:18, Christ "was made alive in the spirit," thus emphasizing that bodily death is not the end because Christ *was* alive.

Before proceeding, let us add another element of context—anticipation of the end times. The writer of 1 Peter stresses to the readers to be diligent in obeying God, suggesting the last days are imminent. "Therefore prepare your minds for action; discipline yourselves; set all your hope on the grace that Jesus Christ will bring you when he is revealed. Like obedient children, do not be conformed to the desires that you formerly had in ignorance" (1 Pet 1:13–14 NRSV). Here is another direct reference: "The end of all things is near. Therefore be alert and of sober mind so that you may pray" (1 Pet 4:7 NRSV). Other verses could be cited: 2:12, 4:17–18, and 5:4.

The idea of the end times would be comparable to the days of Noah while God waited patiently. All but eight humans died in the Flood, and those who died were disobedient. As it was in the days of Noah, so it was in the days when 1 Peter was written. God was waiting patiently. The readers themselves, who had been disobedient, were saved—analogously to the eight persons God saved in the ark. The readers were saved by water baptism—"through the resurrection of Jesus Christ" (1 Pet 3:21 NRSV)—and they now have the opportunity to demonstrate their obedience to God.

Now, we can consider the meaning of 1 Peter 3:18–20. If the text means that Christ preached a message of salvation to people who had died during the Flood, the original readers of 1 Peter would have been greatly encouraged—they would have known that their own family members such as parents, grandparents, and even more distant ancestors who had already died while being disobedient to God could be saved by Christ, as were the disobedient in the days of Noah. For this potential conclusion, we need to keep in mind that 1 Peter was written to former pagans, probably most of whom were first-generation Christians. The new Christians still lived among pagans, and knowing that the power of Christ could save their family members and friends would have been a tremendous encouragement to follow in the way of Christ. Even after his crucifixion, Jesus was not idle, but was active in saving souls.

Another possible interpretation of verse 3:19 is that Christ made proclamation to evil angelic spirits, rather than or in addition to human spirits. Much scholarly work has been developed to support this position.[60] In this case, knowing of Christ's proclamation to the evil angelic spirits would have bolstered the readers' confidence that Christ has authority even over evil spirits. As new Christians in a pagan society, they would be well aware of beliefs in pagan gods and spiritual rituals. The authority of Christ is also affirmed unambiguously when the letter states that Jesus Christ "who has gone into heaven and is at the right hand of God, with angels, authorities, and powers made subject to him" (1 Pet 3:22 NRSV).

The final verse of 1 Peter 3:18—4:6 enlarges the picture, while at the same time bringing it into sharper focus. Here is 1 Peter 4:6:

> For this is the reason the gospel was proclaimed even to the dead,
> so that, though they had been judged in the flesh as everyone is
> judged, they might live in the spirit as God does. (1 Pet 4:6 NRSV)

The gospel was preached even to the dead for the reason that though they are judged in the flesh, they might live in the spirit by God's will. In addition to expanding the idea initiated in 1 Peter 3:19 of *preaching to the spirits in prison*, the 4:6 *preaching to those now dead* amplifies the meaning of the verse preceding it. "But they [pagans] will have to give account to him who is ready to judge the living and the dead" (1 Pet 4:5 NRSV). Possible interpretations of 4:6 include that the gospel was preached (1) to everyone who died before the gospel came in the person of Jesus Christ or (2) to followers of Christ who died *after* believing the gospel message. Additionally, the former suggests that the gospel will be preached to all persons of all eras. Furthermore, this verse concludes the line of thought beginning with 3:18 "For Christ also suffered for sins once for all," which is a high point of the entire letter.

Church Fathers on the descent of Christ into hell.

The views of the church fathers on this topic were varied as we observed that they were on eternal life and eternal punishment. This is no coincidence because the topics are intertwined. Some church fathers view Jesus'

---

60. Ramelli, *The Christian Doctrine of the Apokatastasis.*

descent as effective for the salvation of souls, whereas others do not see a salvation purpose in the event. Church fathers in Western Christianity were less likely to see a salvation purpose in Jesus' descent than those in Eastern Christianity. "Eastern Christian authors of the of the second and third centuries—including Polycarp of Smyrna, Ignatius of Antioch, Hermas, Justin, Melito of Sardis, Hyppolitus of Rome, Irenaeus of Lyons, Clement of Alexandria, and Origen—make reference to the descent of Christ into Hades and to his raising the dead."[61] The nature and extent of salvation that resulted from Jesus' descent varies according to the views expressed by each Church Father. Viewing Jesus' descent into hell as serving a salvation purpose continued with many Church Fathers of the Fourth Century, including: St Athanasius of Alexandria; the author of the homily "On the Soul, Body, and Passions of Our Lord," possibly St Alexander of Alexandria; the Apostle Thaddeus; St Basil the Great; St Gregory Nazianzen; St Gregory of Nyssa; St Amphilochius of Iconium; St John Chrysostom; St Epiphanius of Cyprus; Jacob Aphrahat; and St Ephrem the Syrian.[62]

The number of Western church fathers who view Jesus' descent into hell as having a salvation purpose is small when compared with the number of Eastern church fathers with such a view. Nevertheless, in a letter to Augustine in AD 414, "Evodius indicated a widespread belief in the early fifth century church that 1 Peter taught about Christ descending into hell, preaching to all people in hell, and emptying hell."[63] Augustine, who was prominent in Western Christianity, disagreed with all of the views of the fifth century that Jesus' descent into hell had specific salvation effects.[64] Augustine's view is in line with his belief in predestination, which we reviewed earlier in this chapter. By aligning with his view of predestination, Augustine could not view Jesus' descent as granting mercy on a significant numbers of persons in hell. By the time of Gregory the Great (the pope of the Western Church in the late sixth and early seventh centuries), the Western and Eastern Churches had diverged on the meaning of Jesus' descent into hell. "As far as we can judge, Gregory the Great was the first Western father who categorically insisted that Christ, when he ascended from hell

---

61. Alfeyev, *Christ the Conqueror of Hell*, 43.

62. Ibid., 52–74.

63. Goetz, *Conditional Futurism*, 134.

64. Ibid., 134–35.

'took away a portion of the lower world, and left part of it,' an idea neither in Augustine nor in the Eastern fathers . . .."[65]

Conclusion to the descent of Christ into hell.

Two important points on the descent of Christ emerge from Ephesians 4:7–10. First, Christ gives grace. Although this idea may seem apparent to Christians today, it is important to mark its significant for this discussion. Second, Christ has authority throughout the universe, including in hell. When these two points are combined, it is apparent that Christ can give grace even to those people in hell. To be clear, the hope of Christ-mediated salvation for humankind is not declaring that everyone will be saved automatically. Rather, salvation can happen because of the authority and grace of Christ. This is good news beyond what traditional Western Christian theology can conceive.

As presented in 1 Peter 3:18—4:6, Christ could have *preached* to human spirits, or *proclaimed* his victory to evil spirits, or both. This event occurred on Holy Saturday during Christ's descent to hell after his crucifixion. It is recognized that there are other interpretations. In any case, the theme of the passage remains clear: Christ suffered and died for our salvation, thus our suffering for the cause of Christ can be used by God to save others. When Jesus descended into hell, he could have preached to all of the captives there. All could have been set free, or perhaps only those who accepted Jesus' message were set free. Since it is inconceivable that anyone who has heard Jesus' message directly from him could reject his mercy, the more persuasive position is that Jesus emptied hell and continues to save.

The vision that prompted my study was on April 3, 1999. It was on Holy Saturday according to the calendar of the Western Church, including both Roman Catholic and Protestant. According to the Eastern Orthodox Church calendar, Holy Saturday fell on April 10 that year. The vision that prompted this study more closely fits the beliefs of the Eastern Church regarding the scope of salvation resulting from Jesus' descent into hell. Therefore, the importance of the vision is not that it occurred on Holy Saturday according to the Western Church calendar, but that Holy Saturday should assume its rightful meaning in the Western Church as it does in the Eastern Church. In Archbishop Hilarion Alfeyev's book *Christ the Conqueror of Hell: The Descent into Hades from an Orthodox Perspective*, the dedication

---

65. Alfeyev, *Christ the Conqueror of Hell*, 95.

page contains these succinct words: "'Hell reigns, but not forever, over the race of mortals'—*The Vespers of Holy Saturday*." These words encapsulate one part of the vision that came to me on Holy Saturday, 1999.

Twentieth-Century Theologians on the Threshold of Universal Salvation

Karl Barth (1886–1968).

Karl Barth, a Swiss pastor of the Reformed tradition, initiated the movement that became known as Neo-orthodoxy. A further indication of Barth's influence derives from his voluminous work *Church Dogmatics,* which was "probably the most significant theological achievement of the twentieth century. Barth did not live to finish this enterprise, so that his exposition of the doctrine of redemption is incomplete."[66]

Christian hope, as Barth perceives it, results from Jesus Christ speaking through two monumental actions: His resurrection and the illuminating effect of the Holy Spirit. People with faith have heard the truth of his message and thus have hope, enabling the Christian to be a witness—here and now—for Christ. Jesus Christ is the very essence of the message of reconciliation, and he has not yet spoken all that he has to impart.

> For He has not yet spoken universally of Himself and the act of reconciliation accomplished in Him. He has not yet spoken of it in such a way that the ears and reason and hearts of all must receive it. He has not spoken of it immediately, i.e., in such a way that even those who are awakened by Him to faith and love can hear His voice in perfect purity and to the exclusion of every conceivable contraction and opposition and above all participation in human falsehood. He has not yet spoken of it definitively, i.e., in the final Word of the Judge at which every knee must bow, both of things in heaven and things on earth (Phil 2:10). He has not yet spoken of it in such sort that for Christians and non-Christians, for the living and the dead, there can be no option but "to live under Him in His kingdom, and to serve Him in eternal righteousness, innocence and blessedness."[67]

---

66. McGrath, *Historical Theology*, 237.

67. Barth, *The Doctrine of Reconciliation*, 903.

Barth notes that we live in the time after the resurrection of Jesus Christ and Pentecost, yet before the full revelation of Christ. As a result, Christians can be certain of the first two revelations while awaiting Christ to complete the third and final revelation. During this time, although the believer is part of the Christian community, he or she is still spiritually separated from the majority in the world. In addition, even with solid faith in Jesus Christ, the believer may be unsure of his or her own motives and actions. Finally, until Jesus Christ speaks as Judge and gives His final Word, no Christian can assert that his or her service is pleasing to God. As cited by John C. McDowell, "Barth's hope . . . has to do primarily with the *futurity of Jesus Christ*; the fulfillment of Jesus Christ as the One *in us*; the promise of even more to come. . . ."[68]

Barth wonders what impact can be expected from the relatively small Christian witness in the world. The vast waywardness of the world is easily observed and seems to continue largely unabated. Yet, as God's messengers, we believe that God (not us) reveals the message to whom God will. These conditions raise questions which apply through all the ages. "And what are we to say concerning the countless multitudes who either *ante* or *post Christum natum* have had no opportunity to hear this witness? . . . The Christian is merely burying his head in the sand if he is not disturbed by these questions and does not find his whole ministry of witness challenged by them."[69] Moreover, when Christians withdraw from their witness to Christ and become isolated unto themselves or their own Christian fellowships, the Christian witness of God's message would be hindered.

Given these circumstances and questions, what is the Christian to do? Barth's answer—to hope—seems overly simplistic, yet it has a depth that extends beyond much Christian teaching.

> The meaningful thing which he is permitted and commanded and liberated to do in face of it is as a Christian, and therefore unambiguously and unfalteringly, to hope, i.e., in face of what seems by human reckoning to be an unreachable majority to count upon it quite unconditionally that Jesus Christ has risen for each and every one of this majority too; that His Word as the Word of reconciliation enacted in Him is spoken for them as it is spoken personally and quite undeservedly for him; that in Him all were and are objectively intended and addressed whether or not they have heard or will hear it in the course of history and prior to its end and goal;

68. McDowell, "Karl Barth's Having No-Thing to Hope for," 27–28.

69. Barth, *The Doctrine of Reconciliation*, 918.

that the same Holy Spirit who has been incomprehensively strong enough to enlighten his own dark heart will perhaps one day find a little less trouble with them; and decisively that when the day of the coming of Jesus Christ in consummating revelation does at last dawn it will quite definitely be that day when, not he himself, but the One whom he expects as a Christian, will know how to reach them, so that the quick and the dead, those who came and went both *ante* and *post Christum,* will hear His voice, whatever its signification for them (John 5:25). This is what Christian hope means before that insurmountable barrier. This is what the Christian hopes for in face of the puzzle which it presents.[70]

The Christian is called to hope for the unsaved people of the world, whether their lives on earth are in the past, present, or future. Hope is not a passive activity, as some may assume. With this view of hope, Barth insists that the Christian will be a more effective witness for Christ today.

Barth places the fullness of Christian hope, ultimately salvation and eternal life, in the context of God's reconciliation of the world to himself, already achieved by Jesus Christ. Thus, the revelation of Jesus Christ still to come will be universal. That is, his final revelation will be seen not just by Christians, but by everyone: "indeed of all the men who have lived, or live, or will live, will see this great light, will be terrified by it, but will also be made to rejoice by it."[71] Everyone, including every Christian and non-Christian, will go through the purifying fire of judgment of our gracious God: "indeed to all men and all creation, there will then come the great change of the overthrow of all the contradiction in which they now exist and the necessary bending of every knee to Jesus Christ and the confessing of Him as Lord by every tongue."[72]

Barth stresses that this is not a solitary event; Christian hope is universal. Barth does not say that everyone will be saved in the end. However, he has laid out a set of conditions by which a Christocentric eschatological salvation of humankind could happen. McDowell adds relevant advice: "God's hope for us gives us time to hope for others (and the 'for others' has to be read as having a universal range, following the extent of divine grace manifested in Jesus Christ)."[73] Finally, Barth makes this reminder: "[God's] mighty action on and in man is the work of His good-pleasure

70. Ibid.

71. Ibid., 931.

72. Ibid., 931–2.

73. McDowell, "Karl Barth," 48.

which He neither owes to any, nor comes to owe when it takes place. 'I will have mercy on whom I will have mercy' (Rom 9:15). He would not be God if it were otherwise."[74]

Karl Rahner (1904–1984).

Karl Rahner, a German Jesuit, was an influential Roman Catholic theologian who made numerous contributions to the theological underpinnings of the Second Vatican Council (1962–1965), probably most notably in the role of the episcopacy, allowing the church to adapt to each culture.[75] His longest work is *Theological Investigations*.

Rahner distinguishes between individual eschatology and collective eschatology. In fact, the eschatology of an individual can only be understood in terms of the eschatology of the entire human race. Furthermore, it must be understood in the context of human freedom. In that regard, a person's free will could allow him or her to reject God forever, resulting in the eternal destiny of hell—where ironically the person's freedom is totally lost. Nevertheless, as Rahner views the collective eschatology, he asserts that "the history of salvation as a whole will reach a positive conclusion for the human race through God's own powerful grace."[76] Rahner weaves his points back and forth between the individual and collective outcomes. He warns that each person must take his or her ultimate destiny seriously. "But from the perspective of Christian anthropology and eschatology, and in a serious and cautious interpretation of scripture and its eschatological statements, we are not obliged to declare that we know with certainty that in fact the history of salvation is going to end for certain people in absolute loss."[77] He reaches this conclusion, in part, because he observes that the scriptural treatments of heaven and hell are not parallel.

Rahner describes eternity as derived from experiences in time, but he is careful to distinguish that eternity is not simply an elongated extension of time. Instead, he links eternity to spiritual freedom, which reaches its ultimate fulfillment through death. Thus, time and eternity and spiritual freedom are interrelated as every person makes decisions moving toward eternity.

---

74. Barth, *The Doctrine of Reconciliation*, 942.

75. Gonzalez, *The Story of Christianity*, vol. 2, 351, 354, 358–9.

76. Rahner, *Foundations of Christian Faith*, 435.

77. Ibid.

Eternity as the fruit of time is an entrance into God's presence either in an absolute decision of love for him, love for his immediacy and closeness face to face, or in the finality of closing oneself against him in the consuming darkness of eternal godlessness. Revelation presupposes God's power to enable every person, no matter what his everyday earthly life looks like, to have enough spiritual and personal eternity in his everyday life so that the possibility for eternity which is found in spiritual substance is in fact actualized as eternal life. Scripture does not know of any human life which is so commonplace that it is not valuable enough to become eternal, and this is its high optimism. Nothing is too much for scripture. Since every person is known by God by name, and since every person exists in time in the presence of the God who is judgment and salvation, every person is a person of eternity, and not just the noble spirits of history.[78]

Rahner believes that every person has freedom to make ultimate decisions; that God can enable each person to make the eternal decision of love; that scripture does not, by necessity, rule out any individual from entering eternal bliss; and that every person counts in God's eyes. Thus, Rahner expresses restrained hope, under God and scripture, of the eternal destiny of all persons. Rahner plainly points out the paradox, unsolvable to us humans today, as follows: "Rather the existence of the possibility that freedom will end in eternal loss stands alongside the doctrine that the world and the history of the world as a whole will *in fact* enter into eternal life with God."[79]

This brings us back to the beginning of this discussion on Rahner's theology, now with a better understanding of why he believes that individual eschatology must be viewed in the context of collective eschatology. In Rahner's line of thought, the ultimate destiny of each person can only be understood in light of the destiny of humankind—not that they are always one and the same, but they are connected. Jesus Christ provides the continuity. "The *whole* is a drama, and the stage itself is also part of it. It is a dialogue between spiritual and divinized creatures and God, a dialogue and a drama which has already reached its irreversible climax in Christ."[80]

Rahner explains that biblical statements may at first seem contradictory, but in fact, they are not. For example, we are to love God absolutely, and we are to love our neighbor absolutely. How can we do both? Rahner

78. Ibid., 440–441.
79. Ibid., 444.
80. Ibid., 446.

points out that the two loves actually complement each other. Love for God enables us to better love our neighbor, whereas love for neighbor helps us to fulfill our love for God (although it is not the same as love for God). In many Christian concepts, we observe "the same unity and difference which is found in the ultimate and basic axiom of Christology: in Christology man and God are not the same, but neither are they ever separate."[81]

Hans Urs von Balthasar (1905–1988).

Hans Urs von Balthasar was a prominent and prolific Swiss Roman Catholic theologian and priest. He was also nominated to cardinal-elect before he passed. According to von Balthasar, Jesus entered into solidarity with the dead after dying on the cross. "In the same way that, upon earth, he [Jesus] was in solidarity with the living, so, in the tomb, he is in solidarity with the dead."[82] Jesus' presence among the dead has a transforming effect, as does his proclamation that the world has been reconciled to God. Still, it is through Jesus' *weakness* in death, not the coming victory of the resurrection, that he is with the dead. In this way, Jesus can still reach the persons who have distanced themselves from God by their own choice. Thus, while honoring human free choice, Jesus is present with the isolated.

> But on Holy Saturday there is the descent of the dead Jesus to hell, that is (put very simply) his solidarity in the period of nontime with those who have lost their way from God. Their choice—with which they have chosen to put their 'I' in place of God's selfless love—is definitive. Into this finality (of death) the dead Son descends, no longer acting in any way, but stripped by the cross of every power and initiative of his own, as one purely to be used, debased to mere matter, with a fully indifferent (corpse) obedience, incapable of any act of solidarity—only thus is he right for any 'sermon' to the dead. He is (out of an ultimate love however) dead together with them. And exactly in that way he disturbs the absolute loneliness striven for by the sinner, who wants to be 'damned' apart from God, finds God again in his loneliness, but God in the absolute weakness of love unfathomably in the period of nontime enters into solidarity with those damning themselves. . . . The freedom of the creature is respected, but it is retrieved by God at the end of the passion and seized again in its very foundations. . . . Only in absolute weakness

---

81. Ibid., 447.

82. Von Balthasar, *Mysterium Paschale*, 148–9.

does God will to mediate to the freedom created by him the gift of love that breaks from every prison and every constraint: in his solidarity from within with those who reject all solidarity.[83]

In this way, hell becomes a way for Christ to reach the incorrigible, an output of Jesus' redemption. He became *sin* and experienced the full effects of its horror. "God made him who had no sin to be sin for us, so that in him we might become the righteousness of God" (2 Cor 5:21 NIV). When Jesus went to the depths, hell became his place together with sinners. Nonetheless, after his resurrection Jesus received the keys to hell and all authority over it.

Even though Christ's descent to hell is a salvation event, breaking into the place where no one but the dead may enter, von Balthasar cautions that the scenario described above does not eliminate the possibility of damnation. "But the desire to conclude from this that all human beings, before and after Christ, are henceforth saved, that Christ by his experience of Hell has emptied Hell, so that all fear of damnation is now without object, is a surrender to the opposite extreme."[84] Even after death, there is still human freedom to reject God and his love.

Von Balthasar sees important theological insights from the view of Holy Saturday he describes. Jesus being present with the human dead, even while he was dead, corresponds with Origen's view from the third century. "[Origen] was theologically correct: in 'being with the dead', Christ brought the factor of mercy into what is imagined as the fire of the divine wrath."[85] This view of eternal fire was shared among at least three of the church fathers, as we have seen earlier in this paper.

The Holy Saturday viewpoint also allows von Balthasar to affirm that "Catholic dogma must, in any case, speak of a 'universal purpose of redemption' (ever against the restrictions of a doctrine of double predestination)."[86] His conclusion flows naturally from two conditions: Jesus being present with the dead gives each person the opportunity to know God's love personally, and humans having freedom to accept or reject God's love applies to the living and the dead.

Finally, this viewpoint prompts a magnified understanding of Jesus Christ as Savior and Lord. On Holy Saturday, Jesus humbled himself and

83. Von Balthasar, *The von Balthasar Reader*, 153.

84. Ibid., 177.

85. Ibid., 179.

86. Ibid.

took on the role of a servant—more so than we can possibly conceive. Von Balthasar's admonition seems to call for a prayerfully considered response from Christian theologians, pastors, and other leaders who write doctrines or develop church plans to be mindful of God's purposes: "On Holy Saturday the Church is invited rather to follow at a distance."[87]

Jürgen Moltmann (1926–).

Jürgen Moltmann, a German theologian, does not view the Last Judgment as the *last thing*; rather, the new heaven and new earth is the *last thing*. The purpose of the Last Judgment is not to render sinners their just due, but to establish justice and righteousness for the new creation.[88] Here, Moltmann understands the purpose of God's judgment differently than some view it. "According to biblical idea, through the divine judgment God's righteousness and justice will be made to prevail over wrong and injustice everywhere. . . . God's judgment has nothing to do with vengeance or retribution. It has to do with the victory of God's creative and saving righteousness and justice."[89]

Therefore, at the Last Judgment, according to Moltmann's view, all peoples will come to know God's standard of justice and righteousness in relationship to God and other people. This knowledge is a prerequisite for ushering in God's kingdom in its fullness. "The reconciliation of the universe comes about through the Judgment in which God reveals the righteousness that creates justice and puts things to rights, in order that he may gather all and everything into the realm of his glory."[90]

Nonetheless, Moltmann believes that the reconciliation must be realized through human freewill, because God has created us with that attribute. Thus, God works through faith, not force, to persuade humans that a better way awaits those who respond favorably to God. "The surpassing power of God's grace is not a force of destiny, nor is it a compulsive power which disposes over people without asking them. It is the power of love which calls men and women to faith through the gospel, and entices them to free decision. God saves human beings not by overpowering them but

---

87. Ibid., 181.
88. Moltmann, *The Coming of God*, **236–7.**
89. Moltmann, *Jesus Christ for Today's World*, **142.**
90. Moltmann, *The Coming of God*, **243–4.**

by convincing them."[91] Since God carries out the divine plan in conjunction with human freewill, so should we humans respect the freewill of others, inviting people on behalf of Christ rather than attempting to create conversions of our own making. "Evangelization is an *invitation*, nothing more than that and nothing less. It is not instruction, and not an attempt at conversion either. It is a plea: 'Be reconciled with God!' . . . It is the authority of the pleading Christ, who carries our sins on the cross and with his outstretched arms invites us: 'Come, for all is now ready.'"[92]

Moltmann points out that Jesus took on himself the sins of the world not to subsequently condemn humans. The purpose of the cross is to free human beings from sin and to restore all things to God. Christ suffered and died on our behalf. Thus, Christ is the basis for hope for all of humanity. "The true Christian foundation for the hope of universal salvation is the theology of the cross, and the realistic consequence of the theology of the cross can only be the restoration of all things."[93] Moltmann views two perspectives on God's purposes for the coming end of this world: one perspective corrects the past and the other looks forward. "The eschatological doctrine about the restoration of all things has these two sides: *God's Judgment*, which puts things to rights, and *God's kingdom*, which awakens to new life."[94]

Moltmann is careful to distinguish his development of a universalistic theology from an endorsement of a general notion of universalism. His theology is Christ-centered and hope-based. "I am not preaching universal reconciliation. I am preaching the reconciliation of all men and women in the cross of Christ. I am not proclaiming that everyone will be redeemed, but it is my trust that the proclamation will go forward until everyone has been redeemed. . . . Even for the people who reject it, the invitation stands, for it is God's invitation."[95] Moltmann cannot say with certainty that all persons will be saved, but he trusts that ultimately it will come about.

Finally, Jürgen Moltmann makes this quip, which may confound many a reader: "If I examine myself seriously, I find that I have to say: I myself am not a universalist, but God may be one."[96]

---

91. Ibid., 244.

92. Moltmann, *Jesus Christ for Today's World*, 146.

93. Moltmann, *The Coming of God*, 251.

94. Ibid., 255.

95. Moltmann, *Jesus Christ*, 143.

96. Ibid.

Summary of the four twentieth-century theologians.

Each of the four theologians has developed a theology which advances the idea of hope for universal salvation, although each has come about it in a different manner. Karl Barth observes that since Jesus Christ has not yet spoken as Judge, as Christians we cannot assume what his word will be to us or to others. Therefore, we are to live in hope for all the world in light of God's reconciliation of the world to Himself.

Karl Rahner observes two forms of eschatology in Scripture: individual and collective. Each person's ultimate destiny is connected to that of all humankind. Although there is good reason to believe that God's plan is that all of humanity be saved, for the individual the decision is also linked to freedom of choice. Despite this paradox, which humans may not be able to resolve, we can be confident that Jesus Christ is the answer connecting the ultimate destiny of each individual with that of humankind.

Hans Urs von Balthasar perceives that after Jesus died on the cross, he entered into solidarity with the dead in hell. Jesus did so as a servant, thus reaching those people in a way that no one else can. Von Balthasar cautions that human choice is still operative and that everyone may not be saved. Nevertheless, he sees the opportunity presented to all humans, and he believes that the church should view the possibility of salvation in this light. Von Balthasar emphasizes Jesus' role as servant in addition to Savior and Lord.

Jürgen Moltmann views the Last Judgment not as a time for retribution but for God to establish justice and righteousness in preparation for the *new heaven and new earth*. He believes that God's judgment will make all things right, and God's kingdom will bring new life. Jesus' death on the cross is the reason for reconciliation and for hope in the restoration of all things.

While each of the four theologians has solid biblical and theological grounds for asserting that everyone *can be saved*, they stop short of definitively saying that everyone ultimately *will be saved*. Still, these four theologians have advanced the hope of Christ-mediated salvation for all, and they have set the stage for further development in the twenty-first century.

Helpful Twenty-First Century Theological Concepts

The next chapter takes into account the biblical and theological resources reviewed thus far, considers additional insights, and resolves the dilemma that God wants all to be saved even though traditional theology holds that it cannot happen. Before moving to the next chapter, it will be helpful to review some relatively recent theological writings. These writings do not address the hope of Christ-mediated salvation for all, *per se*. However, these writings demonstrate the need to view Scripture in light of the ultimate authority of God and to re-examine Scripture when old interpretations no longer capture the full meaning of God's message to the church and to the world.

The authority of God and the authority of Scripture.

N. T. Wright observes that God's authority is supreme and the authority of Scripture is a means to an end as determined by God.

> I have tried, in particular, to face head-on the question of how we can speak of the Bible being in some sense authoritative when the Bible itself declares that all authority belongs to the one true God and that this is now embodied in Jesus himself. The risen Jesus, at the end of Matthew's gospel, does not say, "All authority in heaven and on earth is given to the books you are all going to write," but "All authority in heaven and on earth is given to me."[97]

The authority of God holds primacy and the authority of Scripture should be viewed as helping us to understand *who* God is, at least in part and in ways that God has chosen to show us. This in turn helps us to understand who humans are in relation to God and in relation to each other. God is sovereign over the world, yet the world today is bursting with corruption and violence. This picture of the world will change someday, however, when the kingdom of God emerges in its fullness by the authority of God. Scripture should inspire us to work toward the coming kingdom of God.

The implication of God's authority as supreme is that when there is more than one plausible interpretation of Scripture, we should look to who God is. In other words, we can trust the heart of God as revealed in Scripture and through the Holy Spirit. The Bible punctuates the authority of God, not the authority of human-derived doctrines. Just because Augustine's doctrine of endless conscious torment for the lost has existed for about fifteen centuries does not mean that it is the only plausible view of Scripture. Understanding the nature of God helps us to view God's ultimate purposes. This book did this in the section "The Heart of God" at the end of chapter 2.

---

97. Wright, *Scripture and the Authority of God*, XI.

God has a heart for the lost, and it would be incoherent and irrational to think that God's desire for lost people would cease even after their death. God is sovereign and can accomplish all that God wants to be fulfilled. Faith is a gift from God and can be sparked at any time. We see this in people in this life and can believe that it can happen in the afterlife.

To conclude this subsection, the authority is with God, not inconsistent and incomplete interpretations of Scripture. A key consideration is to view the nature of God. Scriptural passages may then carry more meaning for the direction that the kingdom of God may take in its unfolding.

A second narrative in Scripture.

David C. Steinmetz suggests that Scripture may contain a second narrative beyond the first narrative that is given primary attention.[98] However, Steinmetz hastens to add that a second narrative must be explained and must be consistent with, or a logical outgrowth of, the first narrative. The Holy Spirit in inspiring Scripture may have incorporated second narratives into Scripture.

> The second narrative is identical in substance to the first and therefore replaces it, not as an extraneous addition superimposed on the story or read back into it, but as a compelling and persuasive disclosure of what the story was about all along.[99]

Scripture may have a progressive meaning for later generations, especially when considering the synthesis of many books and authors of the Bible.

The concept expressed by Steinmetz may have application to this book. For example, the next chapter discusses the concepts of *two sides of the same coin* and *truth revealed in tandem* that might go hand in hand with second narratives. The Holy Spirit continues to guide readers to understand Scripture while second narratives may have been incorporated into Scripture by the Holy Spirit. The second narratives may take time to discover and understand. Still, the timing is under the purview of the Holy Spirit.

While Augustine derived his interpretation of everlasting torment for the lost using a theology of predestination, that interpretation does not have to be conclusive. Freewill has largely become the replacement for predestination. Still, a question about freewill is: how does faith come about in the individual? Scripture provides the answer.

98. Steinmetz, "Uncovering a Second Narrative."
99. Ibid, 55.

> For by grace you have been saved through faith, and this is not your own doing; it is the gift of God—not the result of works, so that no one may boast. For we are what he has made us, created in Christ Jesus for good works, which God prepared beforehand to be our way of life. (Eph 2:8–10 NRSV)

It is clear in this passage that faith comes from God. While people may embrace faith, accept Jesus Christ as Savior and Lord, and live for Jesus, it is still true that God has instilled faith in the first place. God's role in the salvation process cannot be overlooked. In fact, the biblical theology developed in this book depicts God's amazing involvement in human salvation.

Reading Scripture anew in the time of already not yet.

Ellen F. Davis and Richard B. Hays suggest that more is to be *discovered* in Scripture through the guidance of the Holy Spirit, particularly in the era we live:

> We live in the tension between the "already" and the "not yet" of the kingdom of God; consequently, Scripture calls the church to ongoing discernment, to continually fresh rereadings of the text in light of the Holy Spirit's ongoing work in the world.[100]

Jesus Christ paid for our place in the kingdom of God by his death on the cross and resurrection from the grave. His sacrifice and victory have *already* happened. Yet we do *not yet* experience the fullness of the kingdom of God. Thus, we live in the age of the *already but not yet*. As Christians, we experience the joy and peace of salvation and living in the Spirit; however, there will be complete bliss when the kingdom of God is fulfilled. So we have hope in what God will do for us and others. We look forward to God's kingdom where we will enjoy fellowship in the presence of God.

This book has been carefully developed to make proper use of Scripture. It does not claim to be the only possible interpretation of Scripture, as traditional theology does. Nonetheless, this book has produced a plausible biblical theology. The April 3, 1999, revelation could not have come to me except by the Holy Spirit because that is the only way to explain the insights on a subject that I previously only vaguely understood. Furthermore, the only way to explain the journey of seeking truth is by the guidance of the Holy Spirit. This speaks to the continued prompting of the Holy Spirit and

---

100. Davis and Hays, *The Art of Reading Scripture*, 5.

fresh rereadings of Scripture, as advocated by Davis and Hays, in the time between the already and the not yet.

With all of the understanding gained in the first three chapters, we are now ready to continue the development of a biblical theology in the next chapter. In doing so, we must seek understanding from the Holy Spirit in this time between the already and the not yet. We know that Christ already died for our sins, but we do not yet know the full implication of Jesus' sacrifice and mediation.

4

Christ-Mediated Salvation in Life and Afterlife Resolves the Dilemma

THIS CHAPTER PRESENTS A biblical theology to explain how the hope of Christ-mediated salvation for all operates credibly and soundly within the framework and meaning of the Bible. We will start with the biblical passage in which the Son of Man separates the people as a shepherd separates sheep from goats. The passage is frequently referenced by traditional theology as evidence for *everlasting* punishment. However, the hope of Christ-mediated salvation for all demonstrates that all can be saved according to God's desire and God's word.

> When the Son of Man comes in his glory, and all the angels with him, then he will sit on the throne of his glory. All the nations will be gathered before him, and he will separate people one from another as a shepherd separates the sheep from the goats, and he will put the sheep at his right hand and the goats at the left. Then the king will say to those at his right hand, "Come, you that are blessed by my Father, inherit the kingdom prepared for you from the foundation of the world; for I was hungry and you gave me food, I was thirsty and you gave me something to drink, I was a stranger and you welcomed me, I was naked and you gave me clothing, I was sick and you took care of me, I was in prison and you visited me." Then the righteous will answer him, "Lord, when was it that we saw you hungry and gave you food, or thirsty and gave you something to drink? And when was it that we saw you a stranger and welcomed you, or naked and gave you clothing? And when was it that we saw you sick or in prison and visited you?"

And the king will answer them, "Truly I tell you, just as you did it to one of the least of these who are members of my family, you did it to me." Then he will say to those at his left hand, "You that are accursed, depart from me into the eternal fire prepared for the devil and his angels; for I was hungry and you gave me no food, I was thirsty and you gave me nothing to drink, I was a stranger and you did not welcome me, naked and you did not give me clothing, sick and in prison and you did not visit me." Then they also will answer, "Lord, when was it that we saw you hungry or thirsty or a stranger or naked or sick or in prison, and did not take care of you?" Then he will answer them, "Truly I tell you, just as you did not do it to one of the least of these, you did not do it to me." And these will go away into eternal punishment, but the righteous into eternal life. (Matt 25:31–46 NRSV)

It is clear that the Son of Man has authority over all the nations since they are gathered before him. Thus, this is a Christ-mediated event of universal magnitude. Jesus separates the people into two groups—the *sheep* on his right and the *goats* on his left. Another set of people—*the least of these*—may constitute a third group or may be included in one of the first two groups, presumably with the *sheep*. The ambiguous response given by those on Jesus' right in 25:37–39, in the context of the entire passage, suggests that these people were so aligned with Jesus during their earthly lives that they did not keep an accounting of their actions done for the sake of Jesus. This is a key point of the passage and will be examined more closely along with the next point. The response of those on Jesus' left in 25:44, in the context of the entire passage, suggests not only a lack of relationship with Jesus, but also the need for correction in how to love God and people, especially to care for *the least of these*. Indeed, the people on Jesus' left could contemplate and mourn their self-centeredness and sinfulness in eternal punishment. Jesus sends these people to the *eternal fire* (25:41), which is called *eternal punishment* in 25:46. We will now look further at eternal punishment and then at eternal life.

The Purpose and Duration of Eternal Punishment

We studied eternal fire and eternal punishment in chapter 3 and observed a wide range of perspectives of the church fathers—from corrective and restorative to endless punishment and torment. Of critical importance to resolving these opposing views is to understand the Greek word *aionios,* which appears in Matthew 25:46 and is often translated in English as *eternal*. We saw in chapter 2 that *aionios* can refer to an eon or age of indefinite duration, and the following discussion will build on that understanding.

> The question is: What does *aionios* mean in this context? Does it mean "everlasting"? The translation of *aionios* has been the subject of numerous studies in recent years, but there seems to be a strong case for maintaining that it means "pertaining to an age" and often not just to any age but to "the age to come" (cf. Heb 6:2; 9:12). Thus "eternal life" may be better translated as "the life of the age to come" and "eternal punishment" as "the punishment of the age to come." But if this is so, then it is no longer obvious that the punishment is everlasting. True, the age to come is everlasting, but that does not necessitate that the punishment of the age to come lasts for the duration of that age, simply that it occurs during that age and that it is appropriate for that age. Some reply that if the punishment of the age to come is not everlasting, then neither is the life of the age to come. The reasoning here is clearly fallacious, for one cannot infer from the claim that the punishment of the age to come is not everlasting that the life of the age to come is not everlasting.[1]

Therefore, punishment within the age to come could come to an end even though the age itself continues. On the other hand, life in the age to come could last for the entire age, even forever. Furthermore, this observation guides us to consider God's purposes for eternal life and eternal punishment: "Salvation and damnation are asymmetrical, according to Matthew 25: for the blessed, the kingdom has been prepared 'from the foundation of the world'; but fire has not been prepared for the damned 'from the foundation of the world,' so it does not have to last until the end of the world either. Paul and John talk about 'being lost' only in the present tense, never in the future. So unbelievers are 'given up for lost' temporally and for the end-time, but not to all eternity."[2] Thus, eternal life and eternal punishment need not be seen as extending side-by-side endlessly. Rather, eternal punishment may come to its end as determined by God, while eternal life continues on as determined by God. Continuing faith in Jesus for those receiving eternal life and possible emerging faith for those in eternal punishment are at the heart of the matter.

Just as God created the world and the universe, God has designed the ages or eons to serve God's purposes.

1. MacDonald, *The Evangelical Universalist*, 147–8.
2. Moltmann, *The Coming of God*, 242.

> Now even as the adjective 'aionios' typically referred back to God as a causal source, so it came to function as a kind of eschatological term, a handy reference to the age to come. This is because the New Testament writers identified the age to come as a time when God's presence would be fully manifested, his purposes fully realized, and his redemptive work eventually completed. So just as eternal life is a special quality of life, associated with the age to come, whose causal source lies in the eternal God himself, so eternal punishment is a special form of punishment, associated with the age to come, whose causal source lies in the eternal God himself.[3]

Just as God is in control of the outcome of this world, God is in control over the outcomes within each age. Under God's plan, the present age of this world is eclipsed by the age to come. God is at the center of eternal life, and will govern over eternal punishment.

In addition to understanding the Greek word *aionios* as *pertaining to an age* or eon, we have already seen that *fire* used symbolically in the Bible can mean purifying. Therefore, when *eternal* and *fire* are combined as one term, eternal fire can be understood as purifying that takes place within the age following this world. As a result of these and other reasons discussed in this book, the hope of Christ-mediated salvation for all envisions the purpose of eternal punishment as corrective and restorative, thus reforming the prevalent view of endless punishment or torment that has been held by the church since about the 6th century. As we have seen in chapter 2, the purpose of restoring people befits the character of our God—the most compelling reason of all.

Related to eternal fire, another image of fire used in the New Testament is the *lake of fire* described in the Book of Revelation. The devil (20:10) as well as the beast and the false prophet (19:20) are thrown into the lake of fire. In addition, "Death and Hades were thrown into the lake of fire. This is the second death, the lake of fire; and anyone whose name was not found written in the book of life was thrown into the lake of fire" (Rev 20:14–15 NRSV). Moreover, a list of persons with sinful patterns is given in relation to the lake of fire: "But as for the cowardly, the faithless, the polluted, the murderers, the fornicators, the sorcerers, the idolaters, and all liars, their place will be in the lake that burns with fire and sulfur, which is the second death" (Rev 21:8 NRSV).

---

3. Talbott, "A Pauline Interpretation of Divine Judgement," 46.

The lake of fire is linked to *the eternal fire* in Matthew 25:41 (and elsewhere in the New Testament) and *to eternal punishment* in Matthew 25:46. The eternal fire is described as "prepared for the devil and his angels" (Matt 25:41 NRSV). This suggests that the eternal fire was not intended for humans before the fall of Adam and Eve. As cited above, *fire* can be used symbolically for purification. The lake of fire, then, could reflect a comprehensive way of purifying the remainder of sinful humanity that did not accept and act on Jesus' redemption for them. Although the image of a lake suggests a collective purification, it is also a proper image for individual purification. The second death is a spiritual death, from which comes a new birth. It must be remembered that people in the lake of fire have never experienced a spiritual rebirth. They have died physically but not spiritually. Alternatively, those who enter eternal life without eternal punishment died spiritually and were born again while on earth.

Those people whose names are not written in the book of life are thrown into the lake of fire. There, they will experience purification. These people's names could then be added after they accept Jesus Christ as Savior and Lord, repent, and experience purification. Another explanation is that a new name is given to those who overcome, and this new name is in the book of life, whereas the old name associated with one's sinful self is not in the book of life.[4] The persons with sinful patterns will enter eternal life but not with the sinfulness they exhibited on earth: *cowardly, faithless, polluted, murderers, fornicators, sorcerers, idolaters, and liars*. They will enter eternal life as transformed persons devoted to Christ and his kingdom.

This purification process cleanses the person of sin while preserving the person himself or herself and importantly the image of God within each person.

> But just what is it, I ask, that the lake of fire finally consumes and destroys? It could hardly be the image of God that remains in even the worse of sinners, nor could it be the 'vessel of mercy' that God 'has prepared beforehand for glory'. It is instead the flesh, the sinful nature, the false self that the lake of fire finally consumes and destroys. For the whole point of fire as an image is that fire consumes something, and throughout the Bible, therefore, fire is a symbol of both judgement and purification, two sides of the same coin.[5]

4. Ibid., 42.
5. Ibid.

The point of correction or purifying in the afterlife is to show the person the need to repent of his or her sins and turn to God. In addition, since the image of God remains in each person through the eternal fire, there is divinely-placed hope and resilience within everyone. The process is guided by God in love, which in earthly terms, we may think of as something akin to a concerned parent's *tough love*. It is not to be taken lightly, for it may involve anguish and remorse before repentance. Still, God has dominion over hell, using it or the lake of fire to bring about correction and redemption, not endless torment.

Purifying does not repeat what Jesus Christ has already done on the cross, for Jesus atoned for the sins of everyone in the world. Purifying and repentance in the afterlife follow the same process as when God invites a person by grace to salvation during this lifetime: the new believer responds through faith, believes in Jesus Christ, and repents—turning away from his or her sins and toward God. The Holy Spirit continues to guide the person in sanctification. Whether during this lifetime or in the afterlife, the goal for each person is to become Christ-like, offer praise to God, receive eternal life, and continue in holy living.

Although the purifying process may seem to the person to continue without end—regardless of the length of its actual duration for each person—eternal punishment for each person comes to completion within the age. The Bible speaks of ages, such as in this passage in Ephesians, which specifically refers to *this age* and *the age to come*. "God put this power to work in Christ when he raised him from the dead and seated him at his right hand in the heavenly places, far above all rule and authority and power and dominion, and above every name that is named, not only *in this age but also in the age to come*" (Eph 1:20–21 NRSV, *emphasis added*). As a result of the resurrection of Christ and his ascension to the Father, Christ has authority over all powers continuing *in the age to come*. Thus, Christ is at the center of salvation in the afterlife as well as the present age.

Understanding the *Mystery of Christ*— from Paul until Now

As we read further in Ephesians, chapter 3, Paul is speaking of the mystery that had become known through his calling whereby the Gentiles were included as *fellow heirs* with Jews. The mystery had been "hidden for *ages* in God *who created all things*" (Eph 3:9 NRSV, *emphases added*). Think of the various reactions of first century Jewish Christians to this pronouncement! Similarly, it is understandable that twenty-first century Christians who have heard only traditional theology (including endless conscious punishment) may be skeptical initially of the hope of Christ-mediated salvation for all. Still, there is a connection, or a progression, to the revelation of *the mystery of Christ* described in the following passage, which presents God's plan for the Gentiles revealed to Paul and then others.

> This is the reason that I Paul am a prisoner for Christ Jesus for the sake of you Gentiles—for surely you have already heard of the commission of God's grace that was given me for you, and how the mystery was made known to me by revelation, as I wrote above in a few words, a reading of which will enable you to perceive my understanding of the mystery of Christ. In former generations this mystery was not made known to humankind, as it has now been revealed to his holy apostles and prophets by the Spirit: that is, the Gentiles have become fellow heirs, members of the same body, and sharers in the promise in Christ Jesus through the gospel. Of this gospel I have become a servant according to the gift of God's grace that was given me by the working of his power. Although I am the very least of all the saints, this grace was given to me to bring to the Gentiles the news of the boundless riches of Christ, and to make everyone see what is the plan of the mystery hidden for ages in God who created all things; so that through the church the wisdom of God in its rich variety might now be made known to the rulers and authorities in the heavenly places. This was in accordance with the eternal purpose that he has carried out in Christ Jesus our Lord, in whom we have access to God in boldness and confidence through faith in him. I pray therefore that you may not lose heart over my sufferings for you; they are your glory. (Eph 3:1–13 NRSV)

Directly relevant to this discussion is the inclusion of Gentiles as Jesus' followers. Under the hope of Christ-mediated salvation for all, we can foresee the scope to expand again, until all people are devout participants in the kingdom of God. Also relevant from the passage is that "the mystery was made known to me [Paul] by revelation" (3:3). It was then "revealed to his [Christ's] holy apostles and prophets by the Spirit (3:5). We know that God may speak to the world in any way God chooses, but we may be surprised even so.

Another Revelation

In the introduction, I shared the revelation which came to me on Holy Saturday, April 3, 1999, by which God called me to this study. Now I want to share a second revelation which came two weeks later on April 17, 1999, at about 7:00 in the morning.

Vision of two rooms.

I saw a scene in a square shape, as if I was watching a television or a video game. I saw a room and I could see three walls. No people were visible. Then, quickly the scene was changing, moving rapidly as if down a hallway to another room. Again, I saw three walls of the second room. Again, no people were visible. I saw that there was no furniture in the second room, but there appeared to be things hung on the walls. I was losing focus and I could not tell what items were on the walls.

Prior to the vision, I had gotten up about 5:45 to do my poster "True worship takes time" for my lay speaker talk that day. I finished the poster about 6:30 and lay down on the couch to rest awhile. I apparently dozed off. As I was waking, I saw the vision. I felt awake, not dreaming, when I saw the vision.

Interpretation of the vision.

I wrote the above entry in my journal for April 17, 1999. At that time, I did not know the meaning of the vision. Years passed, yet the meaning was not revealed. Then starting August 21, 2012, through September 5, 2012, I became aware that this vision and the revelation which came to me on April 19, 1999, are related to the revelation contained in the song "Beyond the Cross of Jesus—Christ greets me" (Holy Saturday, April 3, 1999), as described in the chapter 1. The April 17 and April 19 revelations are also related to each other.

This interpretation came to me for the vision I saw on April 17, 1999. It depicts two heavenly rooms, each with three walls. They are similar, but one has nothing in it, while the other has objects on the wall. The vision reflects two sets of people entering heaven. Both sets have already been accepted into heaven, but their circumstances of entry were different. The first set includes those whom Jesus separated as the "sheep" on his right (Matthew 25:31–46). The room has nothing in it because these people gave their lives to Jesus while they were on earth; they had repented, and they had accepted Jesus as their Lord, giving full devotion to him. Their sinful nature had been transformed and they became new in Christ. There is nothing further needed for them to enter heaven, so they are taken into heaven as they are. They will be devoted followers of Jesus in heaven just as they were on earth. The first set also includes "the least of these"—those who are with Jesus and are referenced by him (Mathew 25:40, 45). They include innocent children and mentally handicapped who Jesus accepts just as they are.

The other heavenly room was used by the second set of people, those whom Jesus separated as the "goats" on his left. They have come to heaven from the lake of fire, where they were purged of sin. They cried out to God, and Jesus rescued them from their hopeless state. No furniture is in the room, signifying that it is an entryway into heaven and not a permanent residence. These people will not be in this location for long. They will join the other people in heaven and enjoy the blessings there. The objects left on the wall of the heavenly room represent the old sinful nature from which they were delivered and from which they repented. They have moved on into the full realm of heaven and joyfully worship God and give unending praise to Jesus, their Savior and Lord.

Examination of Scripture.

This insight provides more understanding of the hope of Christ-mediated salvation for all. Just as the Holy Saturday, April 3, 1999, revelation required examination according to Scripture, so does the second revelation. Earlier we examined the biblical passage whereby the Son of Man separates the people as a shepherd separates the sheep and the goats (Matthew 25:31–46). The preceding passage in Matthew 25:14–30 may also be considered as a reference point. In that passage, two good and faithful servants are each commended by their master for making prudent use of his resources, while the third servant is chastised as lazy and wicked for doing nothing with the master's resources. Clearly the two *good and faithful servants* are similar to the people depicted as *sheep* in that they carried out productive deeds pleasing to their master. On the other hand, the *wicked and lazy servant* is similar to the people depicted as *goats* for failing to do what would have pleased the master.

In the next section, we will examine biblical passages which describe people who obey and thereby honor their master, the Lord Jesus Christ.

Scriptural Descriptions of Persons Who Obey Christ

As noted above, the ones referred to as *sheep* are people who during their earthly lives were fully aligned with Jesus. They love the Lord with all their heart, soul, and mind, and they love their neighbor as themselves (Matthew 22:37–39). They obey Christ and follow the prompting of the Holy Spirit (John 14:15–26). Here are other descriptions in the New Testament of those who are *fully devoted followers of Jesus Christ.*

Narrow gate.

> Enter through the narrow gate; for the gate is wide and the road is easy that leads to destruction, and there are many who take it. For the gate is narrow and the road is hard that leads to life, and there are few who find it. (Matt 7:13–14 NRSV)

Jesus is making a contrast between two paths of living. Notice that only a few find the narrow road which leads to life. Also, see Luke 13:23–30 for "the narrow door."

Deny oneself.

> Then Jesus told his disciples, "If any want to become my followers, let them deny themselves and take up their cross and follow me. For those who want to save their life will lose it, and those who lose their life for my sake will find it." (Matt 16:24–25 NRSV)

Following Jesus requires a change from self-centeredness to obeying Christ and serving others, acknowledging that God gives the power to do so.

Teach obedience.

> Go therefore and make disciples of all nations, baptizing them in the name of the Father and of the Son and of the Holy Spirit, and teaching them to obey everything that I have commanded you.

And remember, I am with you always, to the end of the age. (Matt 28:19–20 NRSV)

Both the teachers and the ones being taught are to learn obedience to *everything* Jesus commanded—a hallmark of faithful living.

Putting Jesus above family and self.

> Whoever comes to me and does not hate father and mother, wife and children, brothers and sisters, yes, and even life itself, cannot be my disciple. Whoever does not carry the cross and follow me cannot be my disciple. (Luke 14:26–27 NRSV)

Obedience to Jesus means rejecting sinful family ways and giving allegiance to Jesus over one's family.

Giving up possessions.

> So therefore, none of you can become my disciple if you do not give up all your possessions. (Luke 14:33 NRSV)

Jesus wants more than a tithe, especially when given legalistically. Instead we are to realize that all possessions come from God. Jesus' illustrations of someone building a tower (Luke 14:28–30) and a king considering his odds of beating his enemy (Luke 14:31–32) provide a context. We should not allow possessions to hinder completion of the work that Christ has called us to do.

Identifying fully with Jesus.

> So Jesus said to them, "Very truly, I tell you, unless you eat the flesh of the Son of Man and drink his blood, you have no life in you. Those who eat my flesh and drink my blood have eternal life, and I will raise them up on the last day; for my flesh is true food and my blood is true drink." (John 6:53–55 NRSV)

These verses indicate the ultimate description of aligning with Jesus and becoming like him. The passage presents a vivid understanding of the importance of remaining in Jesus, and he in us, for fullness of life during this earthly lifetime and for life forever with Jesus.

Abiding in Jesus.

> I am the vine, you are the branches. Those who abide in me and I in them bear much fruit, because apart from me you can do nothing. (John 15:5 NRSV)

Remaining connected to Jesus produces real fruit that counts for the kingdom.

Doing good works which God prepared for us to do.

> For it is by grace you have been saved, through faith—and this not from yourselves, it is the gift of God—not by works, so that no one can boast. For we are God's workmanship, created in Christ Jesus to do good works, which God prepared in advance for us to do. (Eph 2:8–10 NRSV)

No one can earn salvation by doing good works. Nevertheless, this passage cites good works as a product of salvation. Moreover, these good works are not happenstance. They result from a relationship with God, and obedience to Christ is necessary to accomplish them.

Obedience makes a difference.

After reviewing the above biblical passages, we notice a distinct difference between people who obey Jesus as Lord during their earthly lives and those who consider themselves Christians but do not live in obedience to Jesus. True followers of Jesus obey willingly, not out of obligation or as a meaningless ritual. Obedience is not necessarily filled with outward emotion. Rather, it is the genuine response of a grateful heart overflowing with devotion to Jesus.

According to the Bible, half-hearted devotion and occasional obedience are unacceptable as an ongoing status. While it is recognized that sanctification may occur at various times and in various ways, what about the individuals who do not follow, or even choose not the follow, the leading of the Holy Spirit in the sanctification process? Does this mean that these people are not saved? Under traditional theology, doctrinal solutions are sought to resolve this dilemma—taking various forms depending on the denomination and traditions. Under the hope of Christ-mediated salvation for all, the answer is straightforward: these people can be saved, for everyone ultimately can be saved, but they will not enter the fullness of the kingdom of God until after a period of correction, while those who obeyed Christ during their earthly lives need no such correction before entering heaven.

The Need for Purification before Entering God's Presence

Christians believe that Jesus paid our sin debt on the cross and that we are justified by the grace of God through faith. Even so, are all Christians prepared to be in the presence of a holy God and in fellowship with other people in heaven? Why do Christians still sin, and what is the effect of a lack of obedience to Christ? If some Christians do not follow the guidance of the Holy Spirit during their earthly lives, how would they be fully faithful in heaven forever? It is certain that humans cannot live in heaven in any condition of sin and strife. Therefore, some means of purification—as determined by God—is needed for those who die but have not fully dedicated themselves to Christ during their lifetimes.

In 1 Corinthians 3, Paul describes the edifying work of Christians as building on the foundation of Jesus Christ. While the immediate context is the role of Paul and of Apollos in building up the church at Corinth, the concept presented is helpful in viewing the eternal value of works done in Christ by Christians, contrasted with works done apart from Christ by Christians. In fact, every Christian has a responsibility for edifying other believers and for witnessing to nonbelievers.

> According to the grace of God given to me, like a skilled master builder I laid a foundation, and someone else is building on it. Each builder must choose with care how to build on it. For no one can lay any foundation other than the one that has been laid; that foundation is Jesus Christ. Now if anyone builds on the foundation with gold, silver, precious stones, wood, hay, straw—the work of each builder will become visible, for the Day will disclose it, because it will be revealed with fire, and the fire will test what sort of work each has done. If what has been built on the foundation survives, the builder will receive a reward. If the work is burned up, the builder will suffer loss; the builder will be saved, but only as through fire. (1 Cor. 3:10–15 NRSV)

The beginning of this passage makes it clear that enduring work is derived from "the grace of God" (3:10). The passage also notes that rewards will accrue to the builder who uses imperishable materials, ones which will last on the Day of Judgment, when fire will reveal each work. Such imperishable materials could include biblical teaching which leads the hearers to conversion, encouragement which helps others to grow in their faith, and godly example by which others can learn how best to live for Christ.

Verse 15 of the passage unveils a triple surprise: "If the work is burned up, the builder will suffer loss; the builder will be saved, but only as through fire." First, some work will be burned up, and the builder will lose the reward (of what could have been accomplished in union with Christ). Second, the Christian worker will be saved—which is amazing and purely the result of grace, given that the worker's output was burned up; that is, it had no eternal value. Third, the worker will only be saved as if by fire, which suggests purification, the method used to burn away the unproductive, perishable materials used by the worker. Therefore, this passage suggests that purification is necessary for some after death. In fact, 1 Corinthians 3:15 is cited by the Roman Catholic Church as scriptural support for the doctrine of purgatory.[6] Therefore, although the purification after death as described in this book differs in certain significant respects from the doctrine of purgatory, there is some similarity between the two concepts. A thorough review of theological assumptions by all Christian churches would aid in the development of theology today, especially in light of the visions shared in this book.

Scriptural Descriptions of Salvation Now and "in Eternity"

Under the hope of Christ-mediated salvation for all, the process of salvation that redeems people during their earthly lives is the same process that redeems people in the afterlife. Christ is at the center of this process, for Jesus atoned for the sins of everyone and reconciled the world to God. The gift of eternal life comes by grace through faith—this is true of those saved in their earthly lives and those saved after death. The people in each group must repent of their sins and turn to God. Jesus is the only way to God the Father.

Next we will review some descriptions of the process of salvation provided in the New Testament. Many of these passages became prominent during the Reformation when Martin Luther and others stressed justification by grace through faith. However, the full meaning of these passages has remained *hidden* for centuries, at least in part, due to the idea that eternal punishment is endless and other related ideas reviewed in this book.

6. *Catechism of the Catholic Church,* "The Final Purification, or Purgatory."

In chapter 3, we saw that this was Augustine's view and by about the sixth century it was the prevailing view of the church. There was no reason to reverse Augustine's views on this topic during the Reformation. He was "the favorite theologian of the great reformers of the sixteenth century."[7] Because the idea of endless punishment (and other ideas) continued after the Reformation, the predominant theologies have applied these passages only to salvation on earth. It may be surprising to consider these descriptions as applying to persons receiving salvation in the afterlife as well as to those who receive salvation during this life. Even so, God's coherent plan of salvation is beyond human constraints.

Justified through faith.

> But now, apart from law, the righteousness of God has been disclosed, and is attested by the law and the prophets, the righteousness of God through faith in Jesus Christ for all who believe. For there is no distinction, since all have sinned and fall short of the glory of God. (Rom 3:21–23 NRSV)

All have sinned and righteousness comes from God in the same way for all sinners—through faith. For those without saving faith in this lifetime, they may receive faith and believe in the afterlife.

Justification by God's grace.

> They are now justified by his grace as a gift, through the redemption that is in Christ Jesus, whom God put forward as a sacrifice of atonement by his blood, effective through faith. (Rom 3:24–25 NRSV)

All sinners are justified by God's grace accomplished through Jesus' death and resurrection. God's intention that all be saved is reflected by the gift of grace to all. While redemption was made possible for all, it becomes *effective through faith* for some in this lifetime and for others in the afterlife.

---

7. Gonzalez, *The Story of Christianity*, vol. 1, 216.

Gentiles justified by faith.

> And the scripture, foreseeing that God would justify the Gentiles
> by faith, declared the gospel beforehand to Abraham, saying, "All
> the Gentiles shall be blessed in you." (Gal 3:8 NRSV)

God's plan to broaden the blessing to all Gentiles through justification by faith is clearly seen in this passage. Paul's message may have related directly to his day, whereas the fullness of this blessing will come about when all have received Christ through faith, whether in this lifetime or the next. While traditional theology has clouded this picture, the hope of Christ-mediated salvation for all is a reasonable conclusion to this expansion of justification by faith.

Born again or born from above.

In response to comments made by Nicodemus, Jesus described what it means to be born of the Spirit.

> Jesus answered him, "Very truly, I tell you, no one can see the king-
> dom of God without being born from above." Nicodemus said to
> him, "How can anyone be born after having grown old? Can one
> enter a second time into the mother's womb and be born?" Jesus
> answered, "Very truly, I tell you, no one can enter the kingdom
> of God without being born of water and Spirit. What is born of
> the flesh is flesh, and what is born of the Spirit is spirit. Do not be
> astonished that I said to you, 'You must be born from above.' The
> wind blows where it chooses, and you hear the sound of it, but you
> do not know where it comes from or where it goes. So it is with
> everyone who is born of the Spirit." (John 3:3–8 NRSV)

Being *born again* is such a common phrase used in Christianity to describe a salvation experience during this earthly lifetime. It may be difficult to realize that being born again would occur in the afterlife as an extension of the same salvation process ordained by God. The person who dies physically but without spiritual rebirth during this lifetime would be *born again* spiritually after receiving divine correction and dying to self during the age to come. As suggested by the metaphor of the wind and being born from above, we cannot see all of the elements and directions which God uses to bring about salvation for each person, who is in truth *born of the Spirit.*

Eternal life for those who believe.

> For God so loved the world that he gave his only Son, so that everyone who believes in him may not perish but may have eternal life. Indeed, God did not send the Son into the world to condemn the world, but in order that the world might be saved through him. Those who believe in him are not condemned; but those who do not believe are condemned already, because they have not believed in the name of the only Son of God. (John 3:14–18 NRSV)

Perhaps the most well-known verse in the Bible, John 3:16 speaks of God's great love for the world, that is, the people of the world. Belief in the Son brings eternal life. Noteworthy is that there is no *time* constraint specified for people to believe. Also, noteworthy is the phrase *may not perish*—traditional theology holds to endless punishment or torment, not perishing. The passage indicates that God values human beings so much so that God sent the Son into the world. Moreover, the purpose is not to condemn the world but to save the world. Those who do not believe are condemned, but there is no reason stated that they must remain in that state. Therefore, in keeping with the whole tone and message of this passage, we can see that it can line up with the hope of Christ-mediated salvation for all, both in this lifetime and the afterlife. Belief in Jesus Christ is an essential element of salvation and eternal life.

All people will be drawn to Jesus.

> "And I, when I am lifted up from the earth, will draw all people to myself." He [Jesus] said this to indicate the kind of death he was to die." (John 12:32–33 NRSV)

We do not see evidence that all people have been drawn to Jesus in this lifetime on earth. Therefore, his words will be fulfilled in the hereafter when everyone who has not come to Christ in this lifetime will be drawn to Jesus.

Saved by grace through faith.

"For by grace you have been saved through faith, and this is not your own doing; it is the gift of God—not the result of works, so that no one may boast" (Eph 2:8–9 NRSV). This is that same passage referenced at the end of the previous section, except withholding for a moment verse 10. In verses

8 and 9, we see the same pattern of the general salvation process—everyone is saved by grace through faith. Then, we look at verse 10: "For we are what he has made us, created in Christ Jesus for good works, which God prepared beforehand to be our way of life" (Eph 2:10 NRSV). Although we do not know if those persons saved in the age to come will have the opportunity to do good works, it is conceivable that they may. In any event, true followers of Jesus during this lifetime are not content to live as if verse 10 does not apply. Anyone who dismisses the "good works, which God prepared beforehand" may be on the same track of the salvation process as those who desperately seek mercy in the afterlife. Salvation is still available but not until correction and refinement are accomplished.

Variance between Biblical Obedience and Personal Views

The ramifications of this theological understanding are significant. Only those who obey Christ as Lord are saved in the sense that they enter eternal life without the need for correction after their death. Nonetheless, everyone ultimately can be saved.

Said another way, some people may think they are saved because they said the right prayer, follow prescribed rituals, attend worship services regularly, tithe, do some good deeds, and even evangelize. However, if they do not obey Christ and his commands in all areas of their life, if they have not truly repented, if they have ignored the impulses of the Holy Spirit, they are not ready to enter the kingdom of God. As Jesus said:

> "Not everyone who says to me, 'Lord, Lord,' will enter the kingdom of heaven, but only the one who does the will of my Father in heaven. On that day many will say to me, 'Lord, Lord, did we not prophesy in your name, and cast out demons in your name, and do many deeds of power in your name?' Then I will declare to them, 'I never knew you; go away from me, you evildoers.' Everyone then who hears these words of mine and acts on them will be like a wise man who built his house on rock. The rain fell, the floods came, and the winds blew and beat on that house, but it did not fall, because it had been founded on rock. And everyone who hears these words of mine and does not act on them will be like a foolish man who built his house on sand. The rain fell, and the floods came, and the winds blew and beat against that house, and it fell—and great was its fall!" (Matt 7:21–27 NRSV)

Therefore, some repent and live for Christ during this life, while for others correction and purification will be needed in the afterlife. The latter group includes not only those who have engaged in obvious sinful behavior, but also those who think they are *saved* but have not been obedient to Christ in this lifetime. Thus, the hope of Christ-mediated salvation for all rectifies the notion of salvation for those who offer less-than-full devotion to Christ.

Upward Obedience

After a person's conversion to Christ, the Holy Spirit helps the person to grow in spiritual maturity; that is, to grow in Christ. This process is called *sanctification*. For the process to be effective, the person must be a willing participant who is obedient to God's word and to the direction of the Holy Spirit. The Apostle Paul expressed the pressing need for Christians to do all we can to grow upward, while recognizing that God makes it possible.

> Therefore, my beloved, just as you have always obeyed me, not only in my presence, but much more now in my absence, work out your own salvation with fear and trembling; for it is God who is at work in you, enabling you both to will and to work for his good pleasure. Do all things without murmuring and arguing, so that you may be blameless and innocent, children of God without blemish in the midst of a crooked and perverse generation, in which you shine like stars in the world. (Phil 2:12–15 NRSV)

Being "blameless and innocent" is an utmost standard. Working out one's salvation is not earning it by achieving the standard. It is recognizing that salvation is only possible by God's grace and then participating with the Holy Spirit to bring it about fully. Therefore, the process involves both God's Spirit and the person who wants to grow in Christ.

The process of growing in Christ should be ongoing, that is, continually making progress toward the goal of Christ-likeness. In fact, the process has been referred to as progressive sanctification. We see this idea in the following verses.

> Now the Lord is the Spirit, and where the Spirit of the Lord is, there is freedom. And all of us, with unveiled faces, seeing the glory of the Lord as though reflected in a mirror, are being transformed into the same image from one degree of glory to another; for this comes from the Lord, the Spirit. (2 Cor 3:17–18 NRSV)

Being transformed from one degree of glory to another describes progressive sanctification. We can see the glory of the Lord, although with incomplete clarity, and are being transformed by the ministry of the Holy Spirit. What is more, the Holy Spirit has given us the freedom to participate in this process. Therefore, Christians have no hindrances in this transformation process unless it is by our own unwillingness and resistance. Another passage shows how purposefully God has arranged all things for our good, to be conformed to the image of His Son.

> We know that all things work together for good for those who love God, who are called according to his purpose. For those whom he foreknew he also predestined to be conformed to the image of his Son, in order that he might be the firstborn within a large family. And those whom he predestined he also called; and those whom he called he also justified; and those whom he justified he also glorified. (Rom 8:28–30 NRSV)

Since God has predestined believers to be conformed to the image or likeness of Jesus, all things work toward that end. Still, believers must willingly participate in God's plan. In other words, each believer must cooperate with the Holy Spirit in the sanctification process. "The journey through life is still far from easy, But because of Christ it affords great opportunities for personal transformation when Christians respond to challenges and struggles with faith in God's greater purposes."[8]

In 2 Peter, the urgency of obedience is underscored with the dramatic description of how the heavens and earth will end; that is, suddenly and by fire.

> But the day of the Lord will come like a thief, and then the heavens will pass away with a loud noise, and the elements will be dissolved with fire, and the earth and everything that is done on it will be disclosed. (2 Pet 3:10 NRSV)

Notice that fire which discloses what has been done on the earth is consistent with the image of fire which corrects and purifies the lost. It could be both physical fire and spiritually purifying fire. In fact, when verse 11 is viewed in conjunction with verse 10, the concept of purifying fire takes precedence.

> Since all these things are to be dissolved in this way, what sort of persons ought you to be in leading lives of holiness and godliness. (2 Pet 3:11 NRSV)

---

8. Wardle, *Helping Others on the Journey*, 18.

If verse 10 would refer to physical fire only, then there would be no direct connection to the encouragement to live in holiness and godliness. However, as it is, everything done on the earth will be disclosed including all of the sinful deeds of humans. Therefore, living in holiness instead of disobedience would result in good deeds being disclosed instead of sinful ways.

We observe that obedience of believers is addressed twice in this passage, first in 3:11 as we have seen. There, the Scripture gives the goal for Christian living: to live holy and godly lives. The unredeemed cannot be expected to live in such manner. However, for Christians such upright living is the standard. The second verse provides more details of the expected Christian life. Now we look at 2 Peter 3:14:

> Therefore, beloved, while you are waiting for these things, strive to be found by him at peace, without spot or blemish. (2 Pet 3:14 NRSV)

This verse does not mandate perfection. However, it gives a strong message to *strive to be found by him at peace, without spot or blemish.* Thus, the second theme of this book is that those Christians who do not "make every effort" (3:14 NIV) will need some degree of correction and purification, perhaps in a manner somewhat like that of the lost.

Growing in Christ is a lifelong endeavor, but it is not strictly of our own doing. Rather, growing in Christ is a lifelong cooperation with the Holy Spirit who guides Christians toward spiritual maturity. Even after conversion, we have free will throughout our lives to participate in the promptings of the Holy Spirit, or to ignore them. Cooperating with the Holy Spirit will result in the upward obedience with Jesus.

> Now by this we may be sure that we know him [Jesus Christ], if we obey his commandments. Whoever says, "I have come to know him," but does not obey his commandments, is a liar, and in such a person the truth does not exist; but whoever obeys his word, truly in this person the love of God has reached perfection. By this we may be sure that we are in him: whoever says, "I abide in him," ought to walk just as he walked. (1 John 2:3–6 NRSV)

Perfection in the love of God is reached when we obey Jesus' commandments.

What difference does obedience make in salvation? It may mean the difference between a smooth transition into the kingdom of God and the need for correction before we can be what we are intended to be.

> Beloved, we are God's children now; what we will be has not yet been revealed. What we do know is this: when he is revealed, we

will be like him, for we will see him as he is. And all who have this hope in him purify themselves, just as he is pure. Everyone who commits sin is guilty of lawlessness; sin is lawlessness. You know that he was revealed to take away sins, and in him there is no sin. No one who abides in him sins; no one who sins has either seen him or known him. (1 John 3:2–6 NRSV)

The expectation of those who will see Jesus at The Second Coming is that they will purify themselves and will refrain from sin—at least willful sin. The strong inference of this passage and of this section as a whole is that nominal Christians who fail to follow the sanctification process as guided by the Holy Spirit will not be ready to enter the kingdom of God without some form of purification that could have been accomplished on earth.

Survey: Obedience to Christ Is Lacking Among Many

A survey was conducted in 2011 by LifeWay Research on Christian obedience. The survey was of American Protestant adults who attend church at least once a month. The results, which were published in 2012, show that only 36 percent of the respondents strongly agree and 28 percent somewhat agree that "a Christian must deny himself/herself in order to serve Christ."[9] Therefore, only 64 percent agreed that denying self is important to serving Christ. While these statistics of beliefs show a deficiency in themselves, the survey reported perceived behavior as even more lacking. "Yet, the study also found less than one-third of churchgoers strongly agree they are following through in specific aspects of obedience."[10] This would indicate that over two-thirds of these churchgoers believe that they are not obedient to Christ in some aspect or aspects of their life. Given that these results are based on self-perception, it could be that an even greater percentage of churchgoers are not obedient to Christ.

The survey presents a conundrum for traditional theology. Do the results imply that fewer Christians than one might expect are currently saved? Under the hope of Christ-mediated salvation for all, this situation is not a mystery at all. Only a relatively small number of churchgoers, as reflected by the survey, are obedient to Christ and are ready for heaven without refinement beyond what they have already experienced in this life. Most of the surveyed churchgoers have not fully obeyed Christ and are in

9. Rankin, "Study: Obedience Not Easy Decision for Believers."
10. Ibid.

need of further refinement in order to complete the salvation and sanctification process. God will guarantee that this process is completed, even if it takes place in the afterlife.

Even though all persons can ultimately be saved, under the hope of Christ-mediated salvation for all, the results of the survey are still troubling. "The survey also examines an individual's inclination to adjust their attitude through the statement: 'When I realize my attitude does not please God, I take steps to try to fix it.' More than 80 percent agree with the statement, but only 32 percent strongly agree. Fifteen percent neither agree nor disagree, and four percent disagree."[11] Such a mixed response demonstrates a lack of commitment to Christ necessary for the effective witness of the church to the world.

With a glimpse into the attitudes and behavior of churchgoers as to obedience to Christ, it is no wonder that double destiny as conveyed by traditional theology—salvation and damnation, heaven and hell, eternal life and eternal punishment—is not as simple as many would make it. Under the hope of Christ-mediated salvation for all, there is one ultimate destiny—eternal life with God—and God continues to work, even in the afterlife, to get each person to that destiny.

Interconnectedness of Life, Including Forgiveness

The third revelation came to me as a vision or an insight on April 19, 1999. At the time, I did not know that it had any relationship to the two revelations which came to me earlier in April 1999. It conveys two ideas, both of which aid in further developing this thesis. The interconnectedness of life refers to the effects that people have upon one another, whether past, present, or future.

Vision of the fabric of light—and its duplicate.

My wife and I were staying overnight at another town. I woke up while it was still dark. I saw a reflection of light in the wall mirror. It became increasingly in focus, which was peculiar because I did not have my glasses on. In fact, the light was so much in focus that I saw what looked like strands of fabric in the circular shape of light that was perhaps several inches wide at the mirror. The fabric pattern could have come from light shining from

11. Ibid.

outside the room through the curtain. However, unexplainable is the clarity of my vision without glasses. Up and to the right of the vision was a duplicate *fabric of light*, which was not as bright as the first.

Understanding from the vision.

These ideas started coming to me in late October 2012. The two circular shapes of light in the vision represent the hope of Christ-mediated salvation for all and traditional theology with endless punishment. The traditional theology will start to fade (at least it has for me and others), but it is not completely replaced by the clearer view of God's purposes as understood by the hope of Christ-mediated salvation of all.

The fabric is the interconnectedness of life among humans, not only those living at the same time, but even extending from the past into each successive *present*. One generation of a family, a community, a nation, or the world is affected by previous generations and in turn the present generation effects future generations. Thus, life is interconnected. Individuals are responsible for their own actions, but they have been influenced by a larger context. A scriptural principle is at work:

> The Lord passed before him [Moses], and proclaimed, "The Lord, the Lord, a God merciful and gracious, slow to anger, and abounding in steadfast love and faithfulness, keeping steadfast love for the thousandth generation, forgiving iniquity and transgression and sin, yet by no means clearing the guilty, but visiting the iniquity of the parents upon the children and the children's children, to the third and the fourth generation. (Exod 34:6–7 NRSV)

Here are four points from this Scriptural passage which aid us in this study:

1. The Lord describes his own qualities as merciful, gracious, slow to anger, and abounding in steadfast love and faithfulness. These qualities align with the heart of God, so important to the hope of Christ-mediated salvation for all.

2. The Lord keeps steadfast love for the thousandth generation—astonishing in number (roughly about 20,000 years if taken literally). It far exceeds the number of three or four generations through which sin is passed down.

3. The Lord forgives but does not clear the guilty. There are consequences to sin. Only by God's grace are we saved through faith.

4. The Lord visits the sins of the parents upon the children, grandchildren, and beyond. Yet, by doing what is right, observing God's laws, children can reverse the effects of their parents' sins (Ezekiel 18:14–20). God's sovereign acts shape the destiny of nations, and God will also spare a sinful nation if it repents and turns to God (Jeremiah 18:1–10).

Fabric displays a pattern of human activity needing God's hand to restore us. The fabric of light also represents human attempts to explain life. Traditional theology focuses on justice and punishment. The hope of Christ-mediated salvation for all sees restoration of all people.

Forgiving Others:
Essential for Eternal Life of Everyone.

The interconnectedness of life can be seen in forgiveness, or lack thereof. Jesus taught his disciples to pray according to what is commonly called *The Lord's Prayer*. Then, he gave instructions about the importance of forgiving others: "For if you forgive others their trespasses, your heavenly Father will also forgive you; but if you do not forgive others, neither will your Father forgive your trespasses" (Matt 6:14–15 NRSV). If someone does not forgive others and, therefore, is not forgiven by God, it follows that the person cannot enter eternal life. Furthermore, there would be good reasons for such exclusion. Unforgiving attitudes would disturb the harmony of heaven. For that matter, lack of forgiveness during this lifetime can also rob the full potential of purpose here on earth.

This poses a challenge to every person, for all of us have sinned and been sinned against. This helps to form the fabric of life, more complicated than we can understand. The sins that were committed against us are seen in a new light, whereby we must forgive as God forgives. We begin to see how our sins affected others in ways that caused hurt. By Jesus' blood, we are healed of our spiritual ineptitude and outright disobedience, but what about the ones whom we sinned against? Does Jesus' blood cover them, also, even though they may not know him as Lord? The interconnectedness of life and the fabric of light resolve this dilemma by requiring forgiveness by us and of us.

Under the hope of Christ-mediated salvation for all, the idea of people forgiving others, even into eternity, holds lasting meaning. People who are unwilling to forgive need correction and refinement. As hurtful and profound as the sin committed against them may have been, God requires them to forgive their offenders. The act of forgiving helps us to understand how God forgives us of our sins. *The Lord's Prayer* takes on its full meaning. "And forgive us our debts, as we also have forgiven our debtors" (Matt 6:12 NRSV). God's forgiveness of our sins is linked to our forgiving others of their sins against us. Forgiving others helps to restore the brokenness experienced by all affected parties. Human free will, along with counsel and help from the Holy Spirit, is involved in forgiving. Jesus' call to forgive signals a challenge to extraordinary obedience to him in this life, which brings forth fruit for many in eternal life. In fact, forgiving can be a sign of becoming like Christ, for it was Jesus who on the cross said, "Father, forgive them; for they do not know what they are doing" (Luke 23:34 NRSV).

Two Sides of the Same Coin

In Scripture, we can now see that eternal punishment has two sides—like two sides of the same coin. One side is that God wants everyone to be saved and that all people can be restored to God through Christ. On the other side of eternal punishment is the anguish and despair faced by the lost and those who were half-hearted in relation to Christ during this lifetime. In the lake of fire, they are corrected and purified of sin, but it is properly called *punishment* from their perspective. They feel God's wrath, which as we saw earlier is not rage but God's purposeful use of anger to direct people back to God. Furthermore, punishment seems endless and they have no idea how long it will last. The second side of the coin is reflected in traditional theology. Yet, it falls short because it does not give due weight to the first side of the coin. The hope of Christ-mediated salvation of all reflects both sides of the coin.[12]

We must never overlook Jesus' warnings about the grim plight of hell, which is so miserable that it would be better to drown or sever a body part if it causes one to sin.

---

12. See chapter 3 for Gregory of Nyssa's perspective on two sides of eternal punishment and God's purposes. Also, see chapter 4 for Thomas Talbott's use of the metaphor *two sides of the same coin* for judgment and purification.

If your hand causes you to stumble, cut it off; it is better for you to enter life maimed than to have two hands and to go to hell, to the unquenchable fire. And if your foot causes you to stumble, cut it off; it is better for you to enter life lame than to have two feet and to be thrown into hell. And if your eye causes you to stumble, tear it out; it is better for you to enter the kingdom of God with one eye than to have two eyes and to be thrown into hell, where their worm never dies, and the fire is never quenched. (Mark 9:43–48 NRSV)

As seen later in this chapter, images such as *unquenchable fire* and *their worm never dies* can have a double meaning. Yet, the lost in hell would only see the one distressful side.

The *two sides of the coin* are highlighted by the following comparisons:

What the lost experience	What God purposes to achieve
Sense of endless punishment	Road to purification
Despair	Dependence on God
A deep cry for mercy	Salvation for the lost
Repents and forgives others	Joy in heaven when a sinner repents
Born again from above	A Holy Spirit renewed life
Salvation and eternal life	God wants salvation for everyone
In heaven with God and people	Restoration and fellowship of all

Throughout, human freewill is maintained. Each person eventually recognizes his or her need for God. We were created that way, but it takes some longer than others to realize it and to develop faith. On the other hand, God is in control of the process of salvation and never relinquishes authority. Salvation occurs according to God's purposes.

The *two sides of the coin* unravels the mystery which has been hidden since about the sixth century when the prevalent view of the church became and has continued to be endless punishment for the lost with no possibility of salvation in the afterlife. With this *two-sides* insight, the church can reform its view to the hope of Christ-mediated salvation for all.

Biblical Imagery of Punishment

Word images are used in the Bible to describe the eternal destiny of humans. For centuries, the prevalent view of the church, both Catholic and Protestant, has been to see these images in conjunction with traditional theology (such as endless conscious torment for the damned). The result has been horrifying images, which have been used at times to frighten people into submission. The hope of Christ-mediated salvation for all recognizes that this use of these images is inappropriate and misrepresents the character of God. Instead, these images reflect God's purposes of justice and restoration that can be seen throughout the Old and New Testaments. This section contrasts the use of images by traditional theology and by the hope of Christ-mediated salvation for all theology.

Eternal punishment.

Eternal punishment is everlasting (endless) conscious punishment or torment under traditional theology, whereas under the hope of Christ-mediated salvation for all it is correction and purification occurring within the age to come.

Eternal fire.

Eternal fire is a specific description of eternal punishment. Under traditional theology it designates endless suffering, whereas under the hope of Christ-mediated salvation for all fire symbolizes a process of purification from human sin.

Unquenchable fire.

Unquenchable fire is similar to eternal fire for traditional theology, for it is taken to mean that not only does the fire not go out, neither does the agony associated with it ever cease. Under the hope of Christ-mediated salvation for all, the point is that the fire does what God intends it to do for as long as God uses it. Fire is a purifying element for the sinful.

The lake of fire.

The lake of fire (burning sulfur) is referenced in the Book of Revelation. To traditional theology, the lake of fire is the form of everlasting punishment or torment for unredeemed humans. Under the hope of Christ-mediated salvation for all, it is the place or form of purification of sinners who were not saved during their earthly life. The fire is symbolic of purification and the lake suggests water suitable for baptism and repentance. The lake of fire may be the post-death confessional and baptismal site, for "no one can enter the kingdom of God without being born of water and Spirit" (John 3:5 NRSV).

The open gates.

The open gates of the New Jerusalem (Rev 21:25) show that no one wants to leave heaven, according to traditional theology. That no one wants to leave is taken for granted, and according to the hope of Christ-mediated salvation for all the open gates signify that there will be more people entering the city after they have repented and been purified. The additional people to enter the city will come from the lake of fire.[13]

Name in the book of life.

Name in the book of life (Rev 20:15) means to be saved during this earthly life, according to traditional theology. Under the hope of Christ-mediated salvation for all, Jesus may have the name added to the book of life for a person who is purified and saved out of the lake of fire. After all, Jesus owns the Lamb's book of life. Another explanation first observes that a new name is specifically cited for certain persons and extends the idea of old names and new names to others:

> According to Revelation 2:17, anyone who perseveres and conquers will receive a *new name,* and that new name is also written, presumably, in the Lamb's book of life. If the old name, the one that the new name replaces, is not in the book of life, then perhaps we all have a name–the old one–that was never "written in the book of life from the foundation of the world" (17:8). If so, then for as long as "the inhabitants of the earth" go by their old name, or cling to the false self, they are in danger of being cast into the lake of fire (20:15).[14]

13. Talbott, "A Pauline Interpretation of Divine Punishment," 50.

14. Ibid., 42.

After repentance and purification, the person could be redeemed with the new name already in the book of life.

Outer darkness.

Outer darkness is permanent darkness, isolation, loneliness, and despair in traditional theology, and these conditions may also exist under the hope of Christ-mediated salvation for all, except they are not permanent. After people in the outer darkness repent and are purified, they may join the fellowship of other human beings in the New Jerusalem.

Weeping and gnashing of teeth.

Weeping and gnashing of teeth show the anguish of the lost according to traditional theology, whereas under the hope of Christ-mediated salvation for all the dual-image reflects regret and then repentance by the people experiencing eternal punishment.

The worm that never dies.

The worm that never dies indicates continuous suffering without end in hell according to traditional theology, whereas under the hope of Christ-mediated salvation for all it signifies the presence of life in fertile soil, which is continually being rejuvenated. From the soil inhabited by the beneficial worm can spring forth new life growing into maturity.

Destruction.

Destruction is used in traditional theology as essentially the same as endless conscious torment of the lost. However, these two ideas clearly do not match. When destruction is applied to humans, torment would not be everlasting, for either the person or the torment would eventually cease. In chapter 2, we examined 2 Peter 3:7–15 and saw how God will bring new heavens and a new earth after destroying the world by fire. Under the hope of Christ-mediated salvation for all, this *destruction* by fire is a purification of the world leading to righteousness. In this section, we look at another passage on *destruction*; the context of the passage is that God's judgment is righteous and his reckoning will take place "when the Lord Jesus is revealed from heaven with his mighty angels in flaming fire, inflicting vengeance on those who do not know God and on those who do not obey the gospel of our Lord Jesus. These will suffer the punishment of eternal destruction, separated from the presence of the Lord and from the glory of his might when he comes to be glorified by his saints and to be marveled at on that day among all who have believed, because our testimony to you was believed" (2 Thess 1:7–10 NRSV). Notice the two groups on whom God *inflicts vengeance* (translated "will punish" in the NIV): "those who do not know God" (the lost) and "those who do not obey the gospel of our Lord Jesus" (the disobedient). The second group apparently knows God, but do not obey Christ. (See the section "Scriptural Descriptions of Persons Who Obey Christ" earlier in this chapter.) Eternal destruction is not specified as an endless condition in 2 Thessalonians 1:9–10, but rather as occurring when the Lord "comes to be glorified by his saints and to be marveled at on that day among all who have believed." Under the hope of Christ-mediated salvation for all, the lost and the disobedient can be saved by God after this event, following destruction, which would mean purification from sin, acknowledged by the person by repentance.

The second death.

The second death is the lake of fire. "Then Death and Hades were thrown into the lake of fire. This is the second death, the lake of fire" (Rev 20:14 NRSV). Traditional theology has assumed that its view of endless conscious torment is reflected by the second death. However, if that were the case, the second death would not be death at all. The second death is that Death itself is dead. The purpose of Death and Hades being thrown into the lake of fire is to burn up these two intrusions which were never intended from the beginning, while purifying humans who are not in Christ so that they may live with God forever. Under the hope of Christ-mediated salvation for all, the second death happens in the lake of fire when the person who died apart from Christ now dies spiritually and is born again by the Holy Spirit. The person's repentance and purification completes this process.[15]

---

15. See chapter 2 for a fuller discussion of Death and Hades and the second death.

Summary of images.

In this review of images, an overall observation stands out. The purposes of God to deliver and restore humankind, as presented throughout the Bible, are reflected by the hope of Christ-mediated salvation for all, whereas the interpretations given to these images by traditional theology seem at times to be contrived. Apparently the details of Scripture have been made to fit traditional theology, even when they do not quite fit. Under the hope of Christ-mediated salvation for all, God restores human beings whom God created to be in fellowship with God and with other humans. The images line up with this understanding of God and God's purposes. Therefore, in addition to the biblical rationale presented in chapter 2 and the theological views presented in chapter 3, the points made throughout this chapter demonstrate that the hope of Christ-mediated salvation for all is in accordance with Scripture.

It is incomparably better to receive salvation in this lifetime than in the afterlife. Nothing in this book should be interpreted to promote waiting until after death to seek salvation and live for Christ. The images just reviewed portray misery and suffering in the afterlife. Living a life in sin has its own consequences in this lifetime. In addition, from the vantage point of the sinner, the depth and duration of correction in the afterlife would be uncertain. Who would want to review old sins and the damage done to others by one's sins, whether they were against individuals or people on a wider scale? Who would want to be corrected and purified in the afterlife in which the person has no idea of how long the process will take? It is not a position anyone wants to be in. Of course, all sins are against God. Still, God treats the person with grace to allow him or her to come the point of repentance. No person and no circumstance are beyond God's reach.

The Dilemma Is Resolved

The hope of Christ-mediated salvation for all holds to the biblical truth that God wants all to be saved. Furthermore, unlike traditional theology, the hope of Christ-mediated salvation for all develops a biblical theology in which God's desire is accomplished without contradicting Scripture. Whether it is Calvinism (which is based on predestination), Arminianism (which is based on God's grace and is heavily dependent upon human free choice), or some related theology, traditional theology does not envision how God's desire can be accomplished. Traditional theology assumes that the fate for many will be everlasting punishment or torment. The hope of Christ-mediated salvation for all not only sees how God's desire can be accomplished according to Scripture, it reflects the heart of God toward people. Other theological systems fail to reflect the fullness of God's love and abundant mercy, and therefore should be reformed.

The character of God is reflected throughout the Bible. "Your steadfast love, O Lord, extends to the heavens, your faithfulness to the clouds. Your righteousness is like the mighty mountains, your judgments are like the great deep; you save humans and animals alike, O Lord" (Ps 36:5–6 NRSV). It is inexpressibly better to believe that God can hold all of these qualities in balance—love, faithfulness, righteousness, and judgments, as well as other qualities—rather than assume that God cannot fully act on them. Traditional theology makes unwarranted assumptions; under such assumptions God would send unfaithful, unrepentant sinners into endless conscious torment rather than provide a means for their restoration. Jesus has atoned for the sins of everyone. Under the hope of Christ-mediated salvation for all, Jesus continues to seek and save the lost. Mercy is given to those who put their trust in Christ and repent in the afterlife, just as it is given to those who put their trust in Christ and repent in this life.

Back to the song.

Now that the theological dilemma has been resolved, let us return to the song in chapter 1. There I described the revelation that came to me on April 3, 1999, in the way of new words to an old hymn. When I had the opportunity to take a Lyrical Theology course in 2010, I searched to see if the old hymn "Beneath the Cross of Jesus" contains additional clues as to the meaning of the vision. The findings are quite surprising. The original poem contained five stanzas, not just three.

The poem was written by Elizabeth Clephane (1830–1869), who lived in Scotland. Elizabeth's sisters found this and other poems after her death. She would have had no idea that her poems would be used for a wider audience, for she stored them in a personal scrapbook. Both "Beneath the Cross of Jesus" and "The Ninety and Nine" became treasured hymns and were used at the evangelical meetings of Dwight L. Moody and Ira Sankey.

All five stanzas of Elizabeth's poem "Beneath the Cross of Jesus" are shown below, including the second and third stanzas that have been generally eliminated from the hymn:

Beneath the cross of Jesus I fain[16] would take my stand,
The shadow of a mighty rock within a weary land;
A home within the wilderness, a rest upon the way,
From the burning of the noontide heat, and the burden of the day.
(Stanza 1)

O safe and happy shelter, O refuge tried and sweet,
O trysting place where heaven's love and heaven's justice meet!
As to the holy patriarch that wondrous dream was given,
So seems my Savior's cross to me, a ladder up to heaven.
(Stanza 2)

There lies beneath its shadow but on the further side
The darkness of an awful grave that gapes both deep and wide;
And there between us stands the cross two arms outstretched to save
A watchman set to guard the way from that eternal grave.
(Stanza 3)

Upon that cross of Jesus mine eye at times can see
The very dying form of one who suffered there for me;
And from my stricken heart with tears two wonders I confess;
The wonders of redeeming love and my unworthiness.
(Stanza 4)

I take, O cross, thy shadow for my abiding place;
I ask no other sunshine than the sunshine of his face;
Content to let the world go by to know no gain or loss,
My sinful self my only shame, my glory all the cross.
(Stanza 5)[17]

The central aspect of theology expressed in this poem is the unique significance of Jesus' death on the cross. Another aspect is human sinfulness, for which under God's justice, no one is worthy for eternal life. Even so, because of God's great love for us, Jesus has provided the way for our salvation.

We will focus on the third stanza. In it, "the darkness of an awful grave" represents death, in particular hell because the grave is called "eternal." The

16. The word "fain" is archaic *willingly*.

17. Collins, *Stories behind the Traditions and Songs of Easter*, 95.

"eternal grave" holds a multitude of people because it "gapes both deep and wide." It is noteworthy that the grave falls under the shadow of the cross although the grave is "on the further side." Thus, the cross envelops both those in the grave and those who see the cross as the way of salvation, perceived as "a ladder." The important point of this verse, however, is its reference to Jesus: "two arms outstretched to save." Jesus is the answer to this most dreaded fate.

The wording in the last line of the third verse is ambiguous. The "watchman" is probably Jesus or an angel. The watchman is "set"—perhaps meaning *placed* or *ready*—"to guard the way from that eternal grave." If the watchman is placed so that no one can exit the "eternal grave," then the poem reflects a traditional perspective of unending eternal punishment for the lost. However, if the watchman is ready to safeguard the way out of eternal grave, it could represent a form of hopeful salvation into *eternity*.

Since Elizabeth Clephane was Presbyterian, it might be assumed that she adhered to Calvinist doctrine. However, it is well to remember that Elizabeth wrote this poem as her personal expression. Her calling was to help the sick and poor, and she would have witnessed unbearable life circumstances. In addition, her brother was a *lost sheep*, both spiritually and physically. Elizabeth never heard from him after he left abruptly for Canada. She was very concerned about him. Jesus' "two arms outstretched to save" could reach her brother even though she could not.

When I saw the second and third stanzas for the first time in 2010, I had already advanced in my studies on the biblical theological basis for the April 3, 1999, vision. I felt amazed that the subject of the afterlife was even considered in the poem. I had been familiar only with the three-stanza hymn. Therefore, the best conclusion that can be made is that the biblical theology developed in this book supports the idea that Jesus can be the way out of the eternal grave.

A little speculation, a lot to anticipate.

Those who obeyed Christ on earth will reign with him in heaven. Since Jesus will be seeking the lost, *mission trips* may be formed to accompany him in finding and bringing back the lost. Jesus died on the cross *alone* to atone for the sins of everyone. Perhaps Jesus will invite companions *beyond the cross*—just as many have responded and do the work of Christ in this life—to help seek and save the lost. Even though the lost will be restored to fellowship with God and other people, Jesus' helpers will feel a certain reward experienced by no other. Perhaps the lost to be found lived across the world in unimaginable circumstances. Or perhaps the lost to be found is a friend or relative, one's own parent or child or spouse. However, the joy of assisting Jesus in bringing the lost back to God may only be available to those who obey Jesus in this life. Whether any of this speculation is true cannot be known at this time. Under traditional theology, one may not even imagine such a happy result, for all of these people are facing unbearable doom lasting forever. Nonetheless, under the hope of Christ-mediated salvation for all, as shown in this book to be biblical and reflective of the heart of God, we may allow ourselves to hope and even pray for the redemption of all.

5

Summary and Conclusion

THE MAIN CONCLUSION IS that the hope of Christ-mediated salvation for all is an appropriate reading of the Bible, and furthermore, it puts to rest the theological dilemma regarding the scope of salvation. God wants everyone to be saved and has made provision that it can happen. Jesus Christ is the only way to salvation and has atoned for the sins of everyone. Jesus seeks and saves the lost—even beyond death—even as humans accept God's grace by freewill. The Holy Spirit is active in leading lost persons to Christ and to repentance by correcting and purifying them—similar to how persons come to Christ in this lifetime.

By seeing God's purposes and God's *heart* in this way, we may note that the church has depicted God in an incomplete manner. God did not create people so that many, even most, will be tormented in hell forever. Some Christians will say, "But each person has but one life and then faces the judgment." That is so (Heb 9:27), responds the hope of Christ-mediated salvation for all, but judgment is for correction and ultimately restoration. See chapter 2. Others will say: "Eternal punishment is everlasting." It is eternal, but that does not mean that it is endless. See chapter 4. Others will ask: "How can a new idea change what has been held until now?" Since the sixth century, the prevailing view has been everlasting conscious torment, but that does not mean it is correct. Before that, the Church Fathers held various views. See chapter 3. These and other issues have been addressed in this book.

Key Points

Christ-mediated.

Jesus is the only way to salvation, and he is the only mediator between God and humankind. By the atonement, Jesus made salvation possible for everyone. Jesus seeks and saves the lost, even beyond death.

Scripturally based.

The hope of Christ-mediated salvation for all is in accordance with the Bible. Old theological presumptions are corrected. Eternal punishment is not everlasting, but it occurs within an age, specifically *the age to come*. There is no contradiction that eternal life can last forever whereas eternal punishment can be completed within the age.

Faithful to God.

Unlike traditional theology with its view of eternal punishment as endless, this book reflects the heart of God as expressed in Scripture. God is Love, and God's desire is that everyone be saved. The hope of Christ-mediated salvation for all shows how God's desire can actually happen within the framework of Scripture.

Hope of Christ-mediated salvation for all.

Life circumstances, such as place of birth, parents, ethnicity, and other life situations, do not hamper God's plan of salvation. Under a restrictivist view, a doctrine held by some churches, salvation requires that a person hear about Jesus Christ during his or her lifetime; otherwise the person is doomed forever. The hope of Christ-mediated salvation for all sees no legitimate biblical basis for this gloomy outlook.

All who have obeyed Christ.

Those who have obeyed Jesus and followed his commands are among the first to hear from Jesus that they are to go into eternal life.

Others will experience the lake of fire.

Except for the innocent such as little children and the mentally handicapped, anyone who has not obeyed Christ will be sent to the lake of fire for correction and purification, under the guidance of the Holy Spirit. In the lake of fire, lost people may seek mercy and repent. Also, Satan is a resident, not the ruler of this place.

Jesus saves the lost.

Jesus overcame death and has authority over it. He rescues every person as he or she turns away from their sins and turns to Jesus as Savior. Along with all true believers, the rescued people thankfully and joyfully confess Jesus as Lord. They enjoy their relationship with Jesus and fellowship with others in God's kingdom.

Repentance is still essential.

Repentance is as necessary to salvation in the afterlife as it is during this earthly life. Without repentance, a willful turning from self to God, people would still be involved in sinful activity. Sin cannot be present before God or other people in heaven, or the bliss would revert to self-centeredness and disharmony.

God retains authority.

God is in control of the process whereby persons come to Christ by faith and by freewill. Under the hope of Christ-mediated salvation for all, God does not predestine certain persons for salvation, nor does God allow it to occur by happenstance. The Triune God persistently uses divine sovereignty to bring about human salvation.

Reconciliation by Christ.

We can see how the world (with all people) has been reconciled to God by Christ (Col 1:20). We can see how all things are gathered up in Christ (Eph 1:8–10). We can see how God's desire that all be saved can happen. Furthermore, God's reconciliation of the world to himself by the sacrificial death of Jesus can be seen as a purposeful step in God's intention to save everyone as is God's desire.

Further extension of the gospel.

The mystery revealed to Paul was that Gentiles were to become *fellow heirs* with Jews through the gospel (Eph 3:1–13). See the passage and discussion in Chapter 4. The hope of Christ-mediated salvation for all is an extension of that mystery—all humankind may become *fellow heirs* with believers saved by God's *grace through faith*. We who are already saved were saved by God's *grace through faith*. Billions of people throughout history have not heard the gospel nor affirmed saving faith.

Diverse views in the early church.

As was shown in chapter 3, there was great diversity of views among the Church Fathers about the nature and duration of the eternal fire (eternal punishment). Some of the Church Fathers, including Gregory of Nyssa, believed the eternal fire to be corrective and restorative. Other Church Fathers, including Augustine, held it to be everlasting punishment or torment. Many Church Fathers did not write on the subject. Therefore, the idea of everlasting conscious torment for the lost was not the prevailing view of the early church. However, that changed about the sixth century.

The view that eternal torment is endless became predominant.

Because of Augustine's influence and other factors cited in chapter 3, including condemnation of certain aspects of Origen's theology by the Second Constantinople Council in 553, endless conscious torment for the lost became the prevailing view about the sixth century. It was not challenged by the prominent churches, either Catholic or Protestant, even during the Reformation. Therefore, everlasting conscious punishment is the view of traditional theology.

Eternal can refer to an age, which may or may not be everlasting.

The Greek word *aionios,* which appears in Matthew 25:46, is often translated in English as *eternal.* Matthew 25:31–46 is a key passage for understanding eternal life and eternal punishment. The Son of Man separates the people as a shepherd separates sheep from goats, with the sheep on his right and the goats on his left. "And these [the ones on Jesus' left] will go away into eternal punishment, but the righteous into eternal life" (Matt 25:46 NRSV). The Greek word *aionios* has a wide range of meanings, from everlasting to time with an undetermined length. It can refer to an eon or age of indefinite duration. Thus, eternal punishment can occur within an age and the punishment need not last forever. On the other hand, eternal life can last for an age and it may be everlasting.

Eternal punishment has two sides.

The two perspectives are God's purpose of restoring humankind and what the person undergoing eternal punishment is experiencing. For that person, it will seem to be without end, but God is ready to save at the right time, when the person realizes the need for God and repents. Therefore, it is like *two sides of the same coin*. Traditional theology acknowledges only one side, that is, the experience of the lost person. Traditional theology has lost sight of God's purposes in restoration.

Salvation comes from the same biblical basis for all.

Without the presumption made by traditional theology that eternal punishment is everlasting, salvation can occur on the same biblical basis for those who repent in the afterlife as for those who repented and serve Christ in this life. The key biblical basis is justification by God's grace through faith.[1]

Images used by traditional theology represent eternal doom.

The hope of Christ-mediated salvation for all demonstrates that these images reflect Jesus continuing to seek and save the lost. These images include eternal punishment, eternal fire, unquenchable fire, the lake of fire, the open gates of the New Jerusalem, names in the book of life, outer darkness, weeping and gnashing of teeth, the worm that never dies, destruction, and the second death. These images reflect repentance and purification in the afterlife.

---

1. See chapter 4 for other pertinent biblical descriptions of salvation.

The heart of God is love.

God continues to show love and mercy to the world. Not only does God show love, "God is love" (1 John 4:16). Love is God's essence. In another related dimension, God's wrath is purposeful, not uncontrollable rage. It should be viewed as a facet of God's love, intended to bring sinners back to repentance. God's wrath is only for a time, whereas God's love and compassion last forever. Likewise, it is not proper to think of God's love and God's justice in competition with each other. God's love and justice reflect a unified purpose, both bringing about God's desired condition of restored humankind. Traditional theology considers God's wrath and God's justice to be evidence that all cannot be saved. However, when properly considered, they do not limit salvation, but can actually serve to fulfill God's desire that everyone be saved.

Obedience to Christ is lacking among many churchgoers.

A survey found that less than one-third of churchgoers strongly agree they are obedient to Christ in particular aspects of their life. Obedience could be higher or even lower than this proportion depending on actual, rather than perceived, obedience. The lack of obedience raises the question of how many people are actually saved. Though we are not saved *by* good works, we are saved *for* good works. "For we are what he has made us, created in Christ Jesus for good works, which God prepared beforehand to be *our way of life*" (Eph 2:10 NRSV, *emphasis added*). The hope of Christ-mediated salvation for all resolves the question. Churchgoers who are not obedient to Christ go to the lake of fire, where they are purified by the Holy Spirit. These people may be *saved*, but need correction before entering heaven.

Forgiving others.

Jesus said that if someone does not forgive others of their sins, our Heavenly Father will not forgive the one who fails to forgive (Matthew 6:15). This requirement could be the reason that many need purification in the afterlife. It shows that life is interconnected and that we are to forgive as God forgives us. Otherwise, the person who fails to forgive others would not be ready for heavenly fellowship.

Summary to these points.

As has been shown, the hope of Christ-mediated salvation for all is an appropriate reading of Scripture. Furthermore, it presents a more plausible interpretation than traditional theology (with endless punishment or torment for the lost). God's heart and purpose of restoring humanity point to an ultimate outcome of hope, not despair.

Truth Revealed in Tandem

I want to describe how the Holy Spirit guided me to the conclusions in this book, revealing biblical truth, which reforms traditional theology. I am calling this process *truth revealed in tandem*. A dilemma that arises from two apparently contradictory (or at least contrasting) biblical themes or passages may be resolved by taking into account the perspective conveyed by each biblical text. There may be two biblical ideas being presented in tandem. Perhaps the most common use of the word *tandem* is a bicycle built for two (a tandem bike); *in tandem* can mean "in partnership or conjunction."[2] In other words, two objects, ideas or natures are contained in one overall unit, purpose, or person.

We are familiar with this pattern in Scripture—for example, the Messiah coming as the Suffering Servant at his first coming, not as the expected Conquering King. As another example, the question how the two natures of Jesus Christ—fully God and fully human— were related in one person took until the Council of Chalcedon in 451 to resolve.[3]

A specific example involves prophecy. Isaiah confronted King Ahaz about his lack of faith. Isaiah told Ahaz: "Therefore the Lord himself will give you a sign. Look, the young woman is with child and shall bear a son, and shall name him Immanuel" (Isa 7:14 NRSV). Due to Ahaz' lack of faith, refusing to ask for a sign even at the prompting of the prophet, the sign foretold Judah's devastation. In the New Testament, the sign is fulfilled as faith and hope in Jesus. "All this took place to fulfill what had been spoken by the Lord through the prophet: 'Look, the virgin shall conceive and bear a son, and they shall name him Emmanuel,' which means, 'God is with us'" (Matt 1:22–23 NRSV).

2. *Merriam–Webster Dictionary,* http://www.merriam-webster.com/dictionary/tandem (accessed March 5, 2013).

3. Gonzalez, *The Story of Christianity: 1,* 256–7.

Another example of the tandem pattern in Scripture puzzled even Martin Luther. To him, the Book of James was not consistent with the gospel. "The Epistle of James, for instance, seemed to him 'pure straw,' because he could not find the gospel in it, but only a series of rules of conduct."[4] James requires good deeds to accompany saving faith, apparently contradicting justification by faith. "What good is it, my brothers and sisters, if you say you have faith but do not have works? Can faith save you?" (Jas 2:14 NRSV). This dilemma is resolved by recognizing that good deeds flow from one who is saved, not salvation flowing to the person on account of good deeds (Eph 2:8–10).

Through these examples, we see that Scripture resolves the dilemmas presented by apparently conflicting, or not completely harmonizing, biblical texts. The problem is with the interpretation, not the Bible. Likewise, the problem with doctrines which profess that some people (actually, most people) will be subjected to endless conscious torment is due to faulty interpretation. These doctrines, which have remained mostly unchanged since the sixth century, fail to see the other side of the tandem pattern in Scripture.

The truth of eternal punishment is understood when taking into account two perspectives: one is how Scripture describes lost persons who feel totally helpless in the lake of fire; while the other perspective comes from Scripture indicating that all can be saved in Jesus. In the lake of fire, the first perspective sees everlasting punishment or torment, while the second perspective sees God's purposes at work—that is, purification for as long as God deems necessary, followed by restoration. Traditional theology has promoted only the first of these two perspectives, yet the second is also found in the Bible. Both perspectives are necessary to represent the *two sides of the same coin*. This book describes how God's purposes are fulfilled by examining both ideas in Scripture.

The truth about eternal life is also revealed in Scripture in this same *in tandem* manner. As an example, justification by grace through faith is a biblical truth. This truth about grace and faith applies to how all persons will be saved, from the most devout to the person who emerges redeemed and purified from the lake of fire. At the two ends of the spectrum are the person who has *died to self* and obeyed Christ and the person who has *lived for self* and rebelled against God. There is no need for people who obey Christ to be purified further before entering eternal life. However,

4. Gonzalez, *The Story of Christianity*, vol. 2, 30.

some level of purification is in line for half-hearted Christians. Traditional theology has made salvation too cut-and-dried: a person is either saved or not saved. This approach can become a formula that expects set responses. It can lose sight of the fact that God controls the salvation process and leads people to eternal life. Only God knows the heart of each person. The Apostle Paul was explicit on this point. "I am not aware of anything against myself, but I am not thereby acquitted. It is the Lord who judges me" (1 Cor 4:4 NRSV). In this book, I have described two *eternal* destinies; out of both, by God's will, persons ultimately can receive eternal life. Amazingly, each person will decide to accept God's grace by faith and their own freewill. In tandem, God allows human freewill, *and* God is in control.

This book shows the biblical and theological basis for the hope of Christ-mediated salvation for all. It also demonstrates how everyone can be saved, in accordance with Scripture. However, this book does not claim that it *must* happen according to how it is presented here. Only God can determine such things. Insistence on its sole authority to interpret the Bible for doctrines that include endless punishment for the lost has been a problem of traditional theology. We can be confident in the Lord, even while recognizing that our knowledge is limited.

Steps That Christians Can Take from Here

It is time to recognize that traditional theology with its fixed idea of everlasting punishment is merely an interpretation, not the full understanding of the Gospel. It is time to reform this theology which overlooks the other side of the tandem pattern, that is, God's purposes of purification and restoration. Seminaries and denominations should undertake an intensive study of the hope of Christ-mediated salvation for all. In order to do this effectively, old notions of traditional theology must be held in abeyance, so that the presumptions which it has held will not unduly affect biblical understanding. There may be concerns about studying the hope of Christ-mediated salvation for all. Some may think that it could result in fewer conversions and discourage Christian devotion to Christ. However, this idea would be misguided. True devotion to Christ is not founded on fear, but on faith.

The study of biblical truths will enhance the vitality of Christianity and the faith of Christians. The hope of Christ-mediated salvation for all provides biblical background to teach about the heart of God toward lost people. This teaching can rectify the false impression that traditional theology has depicted of God in *eternity*. God's essence is love, and God's essence does not cease when a person dies. Instead of telling the unbelieving world "God will abandon you to endless torment," we can offer the biblical message that comes in tandem: "After the judgment, Jesus can still save the lost persons wherever they are." This shows God's justice and God's mercy. Jesus Christ is Lord of all and the only way to salvation eternally for everyone. This is a clear declaration that Christians can make to the world. It properly asserts that Jesus is essential to the salvation of all.

We should put our trust in Jesus, not uncertain interpretations or incomplete theologies. Even though the hope of Christ-mediated salvation for all is more plausible than traditional theology, it may need further development. Nonetheless, two important points have been made that inform the Christian message to the world and within Christianity. Jesus can save the lost even beyond death, while Jesus' true followers are those who obey Jesus during this life. Both points are Christ-centered and in accordance with the Bible.

In turn, two sub-points follow: no one should postpone a decision to receive salvation, thinking that it will be available in the afterlife; and no one should postpone a decision (or rather daily decisions) to obey Jesus during this lifetime. In both cases, to presume that God's grace will be available at a later time when the person wants it fails to acknowledge that God gives grace and we *receive* it. We don't just *take* grace when we want it. This Scripture is pertinent, "As God's fellow workers we urge you not to receive God's grace in vain. For he says, 'In the time of my favor I heard you, and in the day of salvation I helped you.' I tell you, now is the time of God's favor, now is the day of salvation" (2 Cor 6:1–2 NIV). The time to receive God's grace is when it is extended. It may be a very long wait, seemingly endless, to receive God's grace in *eternity*.

An additional biblical passage is particularly pertinent to persons who think they are saved, but do not obey Jesus in their lives. "What then? Should we sin because we are not under law but under grace? By no means! Do you not know that if you present yourselves to anyone as obedient slaves, you are slaves of the one whom you obey, either of sin, which leads to death, or of obedience, which leads to righteousness?" (Rom 6:15–16 NRSV). Obedience to Christ is the faithful response, but to delay can miss out on the blessings of a devoted life. "But now that you have been freed from sin and enslaved to God, the advantage you get is sanctification. The end is eternal life" (Rom 6:22 NRSV).

Christ Jesus Is the One Mediator for All

As stated in chapter 1, a revelation from God led me to study whether the Bible allows everyone to be saved, in accordance with God's desire. I have shared that revelation and two others, which came to me in April 1999, to show how the revelations have prompted me to search the Scriptures for more insights. I did not receive any further revelations until my dream on All Souls Day, November 2, 2012.

Dream of the thin cloud and the sturdy building.

I saw above me a string of hexagonal objects sparkling like ice. It was like a small cloud, but it was thin. The hexagons formed a design, a pattern. I seemed to be the first person to see it, and I told people to look up at it. It was moving horizontally and crossed over the top of a building that was about three stories high. I lost sight of the thin cloud as it was crossing over the edge of the building, about ten feet above it.

Interpretation of the dream and examination of Scripture.

I did not know the meaning of this dream until God started revealing it to me on February 19, 2013. Human ideas about God and life are like vapor, coming and going like clouds. At first, human views may appear sparkling, but can become frozen in time. Our ideas are thin like the cloud. The depths of God are beyond our understanding even though we know that God's plans are well-built.

When Abraham sought to avert Sodom's destruction by asking God how many righteous were needed, he stopped his *mediation* at ten people (Gen 18:16–33). Abraham, called "the friend of God" (Jas 2:23 NRSV), drew no closer to God's decision-making than *ten*. Human attempts at discerning the sovereign will of God are limited. Still, we know that only *one* is needed to *mediate* for all. "For there is one God; there is also one mediator between God and humankind, Christ Jesus, himself human" (1 Tim 2:5 NRSV). Emphasizing that Jesus is human intensifies the mediation between God and humankind. As human, Jesus has personally been in touch with the weaknesses of people and our need for divine intervention. As God, Jesus is able to mediate fully for people.

Christmas 2016 Dream

My wife had a vivid dream during the early morning of December 25, 2016, the day we celebrate Jesus' birth. When she told me the dream on that Christmas morning, I immediately sensed the Holy Spirit conveying to me that it related this book.

Dream of dirty lint and the fabric of life.

"I was in a big, older building with an auditorium and stage —not sure if it was a church or not. First, there was an enjoyable program. Then, the audience was invited, maybe expected, to then take part in a play. During the assignments and rehearsals, there was a large amount of laundry. I was in a laundry room and remember washing at least one thing in a big sink.

"The dryer is a vivid memory—it was huge and had three compartments. I was putting my hand in to remove lint. It seems as though the entire interior of the dryer was covered with thick, dark lint, almost like something you see on a furnace filter. I remember running my hands around the inside of the dryer and removing several big handfuls of this lint. Then, I was going to check down in the filters.

"A woman I know came in and sat on a folding chair near me. I told her 'No wonder nothing will dry. This thing is full of lint." She asked me about a specific woman who was my friend. She and her husband were both there, but I had not spoken to either of them yet. I told the woman who was seated on the folding chair, 'You know, we have had a long-standing broken relationship with them.' I felt like I was going to tell her the details of the disagreement, but I woke up before I did that."

Interpretation of the dream.

I began to receive an interpretation to the dream on January 7, 2017, which was Orthodox Christmas Day. The dream relates to the revelations given to me on April 17, 1999 (vision of two rooms), April 19, 1999 (vision of the fabric of light), and November 2, 2012 (dream of the thin cloud and the sturdy building). To review, the vision of two rooms represents two sets of people entering heaven (the "sheep" and the "goats" in Matthew 25:31–46). People in the first set freely occupy their heavenly residence because they were fully devoted to Jesus during their earthly lives. People in the second set arrive in heaven after being in the lake of fire for purification. The vision of the fabric of light and life represents two God-given principles: first, the interconnectedness of people through the generations and in the present; second, an expanding understanding of God's desire to restore all people. The dream of the thin cloud and the sturdy building compares limited human ideas with the inexhaustible depths of God. Thus, the dream pertains to what has been introduced already in this book and adds more details.

The auditorium is a heavenly venue where redeemed and fully sanctified people will praise their Savior Jesus Christ. The program includes participants who are praising God, perhaps by singing, telling their testimonies, and other forms of worship. The people in the audience are new arrivals and are incorporated into the eternal plans of God, similar to those who arrived before them. People from the audience are invited and encouraged to join in the program. These people, who on earth lacked commitment to or knowledge of Christ, now learn from those who came before them.

Behind the scenes, people are at work performing tasks they enjoy, for example, cleaning. While people are engaged in work, it is clear that God has provided the resources (sink and dryer) and directs the tasks. The big sink and huge dryer are large enough to handle loads of any size. Jesus is the only way to heaven for everyone. People who have been purified in the lake of fire have repented and have left their old sinful nature behind. These people are the second set of people entering heaven, as described in the vision of two rooms. The first set are believers, whom Paul describes as being changed "in a moment, in the twinkling of an eye, at the last trumpet" (1 Cor 15:52 NRSV).

The events of the dream are not to be interpreted sequentially, as we would on earth; rather, they are to be interpreted symbolically. Washing something in the sink is symbolic of preparation for the praise program, like having clean and appropriate clothing. These are images, not actual clothing. The thick, dark lint (similar to that on a furnace filter) symbolizes a residue after the lake of fire. Nevertheless, there is a sizable amount of lint. The laundering and drying reflect that God can make every sinner completely clean and sanctified. The huge dryer with three compartments indicates that the process is completed by the Triune God, in a manner similar to this blessing: "The grace of the Lord Jesus Christ, the love of God, and the communion of the Holy Spirit be with all of you" (2 Cor 13:13 NRSV).

The woman who came into the heavenly laundry room has been a spiritual guide in her earthly walk. The folding chair is significant in that the assignments are temporary. The presence of the friend and her husband indicates that forgiveness had been completed for the broken relationship. Likewise, the sudden ending of the dream without revealing the details of the disagreement indicates that conflicts resolved by mutual forgiveness do not need help from other people, such as a spiritual guide or counselor, in this heavenly place. The dream does not indicate when the people arrived; perhaps they all arrived at the same time.

Examination of Scripture.

"We have all become like one who is unclean, and all our righteous deeds are like a filthy cloth" (Isa 64:6 NRSV). In the KJV and the NIV, the rendering is "filthy rags." This verse may be considered as a confession related to the Jewish exiles returning to Israel from Babylon. It reflects an admission that all had gone wrong. "Israel is totally unworthy, and therefore it is an understandable consequence that Israel's very existence is deeply jeopardized."[5] Although this verse directly applies to ancient Israel, it also relates to all of humanity. "All have sinned and fall short of the glory of God" (Rom 3:23 NRSV). Nobody's righteousness or good deeds are good enough for them to enter the presence of God. That is why the Son of God became human, born on Christmas. Jesus has provided the only atonement for human sin, which is like "a filthy cloth" or "filthy rags."

The accumulation of human sins is incalculable; thus, a big sink and a huge dryer are depicted in the dream. As workers for Jesus, we may play a role in cleanup, yet we will always know that Jesus paid for all human sins, including ours, through his Incarnation, sinless life, crucifixion, and resurrection. We look forward to cleaning dirty laundry because it reflects more people coming to God through Christ. Each person who comes to God with repentance, whether in life or afterlife, wants to be clean. "Wash me thoroughly from my iniquity, and cleanse me from my sin" (Ps 51:2 NRSV).

Turning to Isaiah 64, another group of people is cited, depicting exemplary persons who live for God. "You [Lord] meet those who gladly do right, those who remember you in your ways" (Isa 64:5 NRSV). This group of people is similar to the first set of people in the vision of two rooms, the "sheep" in Matt 25:31–46. Thus, Isaiah provides dual descriptions of people, similar to that found in Matthew. It is the second set of people, the "goats," who are the focus of this dream. In the vision of two rooms, the objects left on the wall by the second set of people represented their old sinful nature.

5. Brueggemann, *Isaiah 40–66*, 234.

Similarly, the dirty laundry in this dream represents the human sin that had to be confessed before the new heavenly arrivals become clean. Such is the case with all people who have not devoted themselves to Jesus during their lives on earth. For those who have accepted Jesus Christ as Savior and Lord, there is salvation. To accept Jesus as Lord means to fully commit to him as Master. Anything less is not faithfulness, and dirty spots may remain.

This dream occurred on Christmas. Let us review one of the passages of the Christmas story. In a dream, an angel appeared to Joseph exhorting him to take Mary as his wife. The angel explained to Joseph the larger purpose. "She will bear a son, and you are to name him Jesus, for he will save his people from their sins" (Matt 1:21 NRSV). What is meant by "his people"? At the time of Mary and Joseph, it may have been thought to mean the people of Israel. After Jesus' death and resurrection, it may have been thought to mean Jesus' followers, in particular Jewish followers. Upon inspiration of the Holy Spirit, Paul sought to expand the meaning to include Gentiles. As we have seen in Scripture, the atonement made by Jesus was for all people. Therefore, "his people" is best considered as *all people*. With that meaning in mind, Jesus became incarnate to save all people from their sins. We have seen in this book how this superlative purpose can actually happen, true to Scripture.

The Final Word: Trust

Knowing God desires everyone to be saved, we can ask Jesus to save all humankind because salvation comes only through Christ. Jesus Christ is the one and only mediator between God and humankind (1 Tim 2:5). Jesus is the mediator of the New Covenant (Heb 8:6, 9:15, 12:24). Jesus gave himself a ransom for all (1 Tim 2:6). Therefore, the continuing mediation of Jesus Christ on behalf of humankind is entirely consistent with the scope of the ransom—*himself for all*. As we trust Jesus for our own salvation, we can trust Jesus to be the mediator for others.

My personal prayer can be the prayer of every obedient follower of Jesus:

"Lord Jesus, I believe and trust in you. Have mercy on me; have mercy on everyone. Thank you, Jesus. Amen."

Bibliography

Alfeyev, Archbishop Hilarion. *Christ the Conqueror of Hell: The Descent into Hades from an Orthodox Perspective.* Crestwood: St Vladimir's Seminary Press, 2009.

The Apostles' Creed, www.ccel.org/creeds/apostles.creed.html (accessed June 10, 2017).

Augustine. *The Handbook on Faith, Hope and Love (Enchiridion).* http://www.newadvent.org/fathers/1302.htm.

———. *City of God (De Civitate).* http://www.newadvent.org/fathers/120121.htm.

Barth, Karl. *The Doctrine of Reconciliation.* Vol. 4/3.2 of *Church Dogmatics.* Translated by G. W. Bromiley. Edinburgh: T. & T. Clark, 1962.

Basil the Great. *De Spiritu Santo* 40. http://www.newadvent.org/fathers/3203.htm.

Bockmuehl, Markus. *The Epistle to the Philippians.* Peabody: Hendrickson, 1998.

Boyd, Gregory A., and Paul R. Eddy. *Across the Spectrum: Understanding Issues in Evangelical Theology.* Grand Rapids: Baker, 2002.

Brueggemann, Walter. *Isaiah 40–66.* Louisville: Westminster John Knox, 1998.

Catechism of the Catholic Church, Second edition. "The Final Purification, or Purgatory." Vatican City: Libreria Editrice Vaticana. http://ccc.usccb.org/flipbooks/catechism/index.html#286.

Catherine of Genoa, *Purgation and Purgatory, The Spiritual Dialogue.* Translated by Serge Hughes. New York: Paulist, 1979.

Catholic Encyclopedia. "Origen and Origenism: Second Origenistic Crisis." http://www.newadvent.org/cathen/11306b.htm.

———. "St. Catherine of Genoa." http://www.newadvent.org/cathen/03446b.htm.

Clement of Alexandria. "From the Book of Soul." http://www.newadvent.org/fathers/0211.htm.

———. *The Stromata* 7. http://www.newadvent.org/fathers/02107.htm.

Clement of Rome. "Letter to the Corinthians." http://www.newadvent.org/fathers/1010.htm .

Colijn, Brenda B. *Images of Salvation in the New Testament.* Downers Grove: InterVarsity, 2010.

Collins, Ace. *Stories behind the Traditions and Songs of Easter.* Grand Rapids: Zondervan, 2007.

Davis, Ellen F., and Richard B. Hays, eds. *The Art of Reading Scripture.* Grand Rapids: Eerdmans, 2003.

DeSilva, David A. *An Introduction to the New Testament: Contexts, Methods & Ministry Formation.* Downers Grove: InterVarsity, 2004.

Erickson, Millard J. "The Fate of Those Who Never Hear." *Bibliotheca Sacra* 152 (1995): 3–15.

———. "The State of the Question." In *Through No Fault of Their Own?: The Fate of Those Who Have Never Heard*, edited by William V. Crockett and James G. Sigountos, 23–33. Grand Rapids: Baker, 1991.

Goetz, James. *Conditional Futurism: New Perspective of End-Time Prophecy*. Eugene: Resource Publications, 2012.

Gonzalez, Justo L. *The Story of Christianity*. 2 vols. New York: HarperCollins, 1984–1985.

Greggs, Tom. "*Apokatastasis: Particularist Universalism in Origen*." In *"All Shall Be Well"*: *Explorations in Universal Salvation and Christian Theology from Origen to Moltmann*, edited by Gregory MacDonald, 29–46. Eugene: Cascade, 2011.

Gregory of Nazianzus. "Oration 40." http://www.newadvent.org/fathers/310240.htm.

Gregory of Nyssa. *On the Soul and the Resurrection*. http://www.newadvent.org/fathers/2915.htm.

Harmon, Steven R. *Every Knee Should Bow: Biblical Rationales for Universal Salvation in Early Christian Thought*. Lanham: University Press of America, 2003.

Hawthorne, Gerald F. and Ralph P. Martin. *Philippians*, Revised edition. Vol. 43 of *Word Biblical Commentary*. Waco: Word, 2015.

Henry, Carl F. H. "Is It Fair?" In *Through No Fault of Their Own?: The Fate of Those Who Have Never Heard*, edited by William V. Crockett and James G. Sigountos, 245–5. Grand Rapids: Baker, 1991.

Heschel, Abraham. *The Prophets*. New York: HarperCollins, 2001.

Ignatius of Antioch, "Epistle to the Ephesians." http://www.newadvent.org/fathers/0104.htm.

Irenaeus of Lyons, *Against Heresies*. http://www.newadvent.org/fathers/0103.htm.

John Chrysostom. *Two Exhortations to Theodore After His Fall*. http://www.newadvent.org/fathers/1903.htm.

Justin Martyr, *The First Apology*. http://www.newadvent.org/fathers/0126.htm.

MacCulloch, Diarmaid. *The Reformation*. New York: Penguin, 2005.

MacDonald, Gregory, ed. *"All Shall Be Well"*: *Explorations in Universal Salvation and Christian Theology from Origen to Moltmann*. Eugene: Cascade, 2011.

———. *The Evangelical Universalist*, Second edition. Eugene: Cascade, 2012.

Martin, Ralph P. *A Hymn of Christ: Philippians 2:5–11 in Recent Interpretation & in the Setting of Early Christian Worship*. Downers Grove: InterVarsity, 1997.

McDowell, John C. "Karl Barth's Having No—Thing to Hope for." *Journal for Christian Theological Research* 11 (2006): 1–49.

McGrath, Alister E. *Christian Theology: An Introduction*. Malden: Blackwell, 2007.

———. *Historical Theology: An Introduction to the History of Christian Thought*. Malden: Blackwell, 1998.

Moltmann, Jürgen. *The Coming of God: Christian Eschatology*. Translated by Margaret Kohl. Minneapolis: Fortress, 1996.

———. *Jesus Christ for Today's World*. Translated by Margaret Kohl. Minneapolis: Fortress, 1994.

———. *The Trinity and the Kingdom of God: The Doctrine of God*. Translated by Margaret Kohl. Minneapolis: Fortress, 1981.

Origen, *De Principiis (On First Principles)*. http://www.newadvent.org/fathers/0412.htm.

Placher, William C., ed. *Essentials of Christian Theology*. Louisville: Westminster John Knox, 2003.

Rahner, Karl. *Foundations of Christian Faith.* Translated by William V. Dych. New York: Seabury, 1978.

Ramelli, Ilaria L. E. *The Christian Doctrine of the Apokatastasis: A Critical Assessment from the New Testament to Eriurgena.* Boston: Brill, 2013.

Ramelli, Ilaria L. E., and David Konstan. *Terms for Eternity: Aionios and Aidios in Classical and Christian Texts.* Piscataway: Gorgias Press, 2013.

Rankin, Russ. "Study: Obedience Not Easy Decision for Believers." http://www.lifeway. com/article/research-survey-obedience-not-easy-decision-for-believers.

Sanders, John, editor. *What About Those Who Have Never Heard?: Three Views on the Destiny of the Unevangelized.* Downers Grove: InterVarsity, 1995.

Steinmetz, David C. "Uncovering a Second Narrative: Detective Fiction and the Construction of Historical Method." In *The Art of Reading Scripture*, edited by Ellen F. Davis and Richard B. Hays, 54–65. Grand Rapids: Eerdmans, 2003.

Talbott, Thomas. "Christ Victorious." In *Universal Salvation? The Current Debate*, edited by Robin A. Parry and Christopher H. Partridge, 15–31. Grand Rapids: Eerdmans, 2003.

———. *The Inescapable Love of God,* Second edition. Eugene: Cascade, 2014.

———. "A Pauline Interpretation of Divine Judgement." In *Universal Salvation? The Current Debate,* editors. Robin A. Parry and Christopher H. Partridge, 32–52. Grand Rapids: Eerdmans, 2003.

Tertullian, *Apology.* http://www.newadvent.org/fathers/0301.htm.

Tingle, Elizabeth C. *Purgatory and Piety in Brittany 1480–1720.* Burlington: Ashgate, 2012.

Van Beeck, Frans Jozef. "'Lost and Found' in Luke 15: Biblical Interpretation and Self-Involvement." *The Expository Times* 114 (2003): 399–404.

Von Balthasar, Hans Urs. *Mysterium Paschale.* Translated by Aiden Nichols. Edinburgh: T&T Clark, 1990.

———. *The von Balthasar Reader,* edited by Medard Kehland and Werner Loser. Translated by Robert J. Daly and Fred Lawrence. New York: Crossroad, 1997.

Walls, Jerry L., ed. *The Oxford Handbook of Eschatology.* Oxford: Oxford University Press, 2008.

Wardle, Terry. *Helping Others on the Journey: A Guide for Those Who Seek to Mentor Others to Maturity in Christ.* Abilene: Leafwood, 2004.

Wright, N. T. *Scripture and the Authority of God: How to Read the Bible Today.* New York: HarperOne, 2011.

Name Index

Scripture Index